# THE SUGAR PROGRAM

# Evaluative Studies

This series of studies seeks to bring about greater understanding and promote continuing review of the activities and functions·of the federal government. Each study focuses on a specific program, evaluating its cost and efficiency, the extent to which it achieves its objectives, and the major alternative means—public and private—for reaching those objectives. Yale Brozen, professor of economics at the University of Chicago and an adjunct scholar of the American Enterprise Institute for Public Policy Research, is the director of the program.

# THE
# SUGAR PROGRAM
## Large costs and small benefits

D. Gale Johnson

American Enterprise Institute for Public Policy Research
Washington, D. C.

D. Gale Johnson is professor of economics at the University
of Chicago.

ISBN 0-8447-3126-9

Evaluative Studies 14, April 1974

Library of Congress Catalog Card No. L.C. 74-78952

*Printed in the United States of America*

# CONTENTS

# INTRODUCTION
# AND SUMMARY

President Franklin D. Roosevelt sent a message to Congress in early 1934 outlining the structure of a sugar program. He said that one of the objectives of the proposed program was "to provide against further expansion of this necessarily expensive industry." Another objective was to keep down the price of sugar to consumers. A third objective was to retain sugar beet and sugar cane farming within our continental limits.

Of these three objectives only the retention of cane and beet production within our continental limits has been achieved. In fact, this objective has been so well achieved that output within our continental limits has more than doubled under the sugar program. The sugar program has failed to keep down the price of sugar and has certainly failed in achieving the objective of halting the expansion of "this necessarily expensive industry."

### Focus of the Study

The sugar program was born during the depression of the 1930s, as were the other farm programs. There was great economic distress among farmers, and actions were required to prevent unnecessary hardship. As in so many other cases, what were considered emergency programs were continued long after the economic circumstances in agriculture had radically changed.

The basic structure of the sugar program has remained unchanged for four decades. Unfortunately the basic attribute of the production of sugar cane and sugar beets as a high-cost industry has also persisted. This essay focuses on the costs of the sugar program to

1

consumers and taxpayers and the net benefits that have been derived by domestic and foreign producers. In the last chapter the general framework of a new approach to the sugar industry is presented.

## Summary of Findings

The production, distribution and pricing of sugar is highly regulated in almost all countries. The United States sugar program is in no way unique. Most industrial countries protect their own sugar production and produce a large fraction, if not all, of their domestic consumption requirements. It may be that two-fifths'of the world's sugar production is in the wrong places because sugar production has been encouraged under high-cost conditions. The United States might be said to have a relatively liberal trade policy for sugar since we import approximately 45 percent of our consumption. But this is only by comparison with policies that are even more disruptive to international specialization and trade.

More than half of the sugar that moves in international trade does so within the framework of special preferential arrangements, principally the U.S. sugar program with its assigned sugar quotas, the British Commonwealth Sugar Agreement, and the arrangements between the Soviet Union and Cuba. Low-cost producers of sugar, such as Brazil and Mexico, have little opportunity to expand their production beyond the amounts required for domestic consumption and sales to the preferential markets since the price of raw sugar on the world market has been both low and highly variable.

There are enormous differences in the prices that farmers of different countries receive for the production of sugar cane and beets. As of 1970 farmers in Brazil and Mexico received about a third as much as farmers in the United States and Western Europe.

An important—and apparently intended—effect of the U.S. sugar program has been the protection of sugar refining. While it may appear that the sugar program is a farm program, it is also a highly protective program for sugar refining. Sugar quotas are more stringent against refined sugar than raw sugar. Currently only 68,000 tons out of total sugar imports of more than 5 million tons can be imported as refined or direct-consumption sugar. Further, the legislation regulates and restricts the amount of refined sugar that can be brought to the continental United States from Hawaii and Puerto Rico.

There are no clear guidelines for establishing import quotas and quotas for domestic areas. There are no rational grounds for choosing between sugar from Brazil or Ireland or Australia. As a result the quotas must be assigned by a political process that is dependent, at least to some degree, upon the use of paid lobbyists by foreign governments and active courting of senators and congressmen by domestic groups.

It is estimated that the annual cost of the sugar program to American consumers and taxpayers ranges between $502 and $730 million. This is an estimate for long-run conditions in terms of 1972 levels of U.S. sugar prices and consumption. Based on a mid-range estimate of $616 million, approximately a third of the gross transfer goes to foreign quota holders and the remainder to the domestic sugar producers.

The net income benefit—the increase in net income of the producers of sugar—is much smaller than the gross cost. For domestic producers the net income benefit is estimated to be about $100 million annually, approximately a quarter of gross transfers. The net income increases to foreign quota holders are relatively small, with the main beneficiaries being the countries that purchase a large part of their sugar in the world market. The two largest such purchasers are Japan and Canada.

The distribution of the gross benefits among farmers is very unequal. Out of a total of 21,000 sugar-producing farms in the United States, 224 farms produce at least a third of the sugar. Sixty-five farms produce approximately a fourth of all sugar and receive a sixth of all sugar program payments.

It is my conclusion that the current sugar program should be replaced because the cost is much greater than the benefit to producers and because it is inconsistent with a liberal trade policy. The long-run sugar program should be one consistent with liberalization of trade. It should include moderate tariffs of approximately 10 percent on raw and refined sugar, and price supports at a level consistent with the expected world price of sugar. Any difference between the support price and actual market price of sugar cane and beets should be met by a deficiency payment.

Two approaches are suggested for moving to the long-run sugar program. One is for a transition program in which the import quotas and domestic marketing allocations would be abolished and a target price established. The difference between the target price and the actual market price would be met by a deficiency payment for a level of output no greater than the average output for the past three years. The Sugar Act payments would be phased out over a five-year period. To ease their adjustment to the long-run program, producers should be permitted to abandon cane and beet production in whole or in part and continue to receive the payments they would be entitled to if they had produced as much as during the three years before the transition period.

The second approach is to move at once to the long-run program and compensenate fully all the losses that would be incurred by farmers, workers, and processors. It is estimated that the cost of such compensation would be no more than the costs to consumers and taxpayers of continuing the present sugar program for four years.

# CHAPTER I

# OUR SWEET TOOTH

"What are little girls made of? Sugar and spice and all that's nice." In this old rhyme, which has quite derogatory things to say about little boys, sugar is given prominent and favorable notice. Until recently, when some suspicion, if not proof, arose that sugar may be an important factor in tooth decay and other disabilities, sugar was almost always considered in a favorable light. *Roget's Thesaurus* gives "sugariness" as one of the main synonyms of sweetness, and sweetness, when not considered as an aspect of taste, has other synonyms that in most settings are given high value—amiability, gentleness, kindness, and good disposition or humor.

It has been said that there was a connection between sugar or molasses and the American Revolution. John Adams wrote: "General Washington always asserted and proved that Virginians loved molasses as well as New Englanders did. I know not why we should blush to confess that molasses was an essential ingredient in American independence. Many great events have proceeded from much smaller causes." [1] Adams's reference was to the opposition to the various sugar acts applied by the British to the American colonies. The duties were considered to be extremely high, and a great deal of smuggling occurred. At the time of the American Revolution the only domestically produced sweeteners were honey and maple syrup. Thus the duties appeared as a tax on consumption and on a product that was highly desired.

American annual per capita consumption of beet and cane sugar now slightly exceeds 100 pounds. This is more than ten times the consumption of sugar at the time of the Revolution. (The earliest estimate of per capita sugar consumption is for 1822: 9.5 pounds per capita.) [2]

5

In 1971 the consumption of other forms of caloric sweeteners (primarily corn sugar and corn syrup) brought the total per capita consumption of sweeteners to 125 pounds.[3] Sugars and other sweeteners now provide about 17 percent of the total caloric consumption of food in the United States.[4] Sugar makes no other significant contribution to the diet except for supplying approximately 6 percent of iron. Only meats, poultry, and fish, as a food group, and flour and cereals contribute a larger fraction of the caloric intake, each providing about a fifth of the total.

Caloric sweetener consumption continues to increase gradually. In the past decade U.S. per capita consumption of sugar rose approximately 10 percent: from 114 pounds in 1961 to 125 pounds in 1971.[5] Due to favorable price relationships, almost half of the increase in consumption during the decade was in corn sugar and syrup.

Americans are not the only people with a sweet tooth. Per capita consumption of sugar and sweets is approximately the same as that in the United States in Denmark, Ireland, the Netherlands, the United Kingdom, and Australia. France and West Germany are not far behind.[6]

Our sweet tooth is evidenced not only by our willingness to consume a great deal of sugar. To some degree our favorable attitudes toward sugar are reflected in our willingness to permit the government to provide a high level of protection for what is generally acknowledged to be a high-cost industry. Almost all other industrial countries protect their sugar industries, some of them to an even greater degree than we do.[7] While one may be puzzled by the tender loving care that politicians have given to sugar and its production, the fact of that care is indisputable.

One could say that the protective policies all began with Napoleon. Prior to the beginning of the nineteenth century the only source of sugar was cane, which can be produced only under tropical or semitropical conditions. In all of Europe, only southern Spain was suitable for production of cane sugar. There was a substantial trade in sugar from the Americas to Europe in the late eighteenth century, but this supply was vulnerable to naval blockade. As sugar was of some importance in the diet of the French, Napoleon actively sought a domestic source. His efforts were rewarded, and between 1811 and 1815 forty sugar beet factories were put into operation. After Napoleon's defeat at Waterloo, the French sugar industry went into a major decline, though it never entirely disappeared.[8]

With the abolition of slavery in the West Indies in 1843, the production of cane sugar either declined or grew very slowly. This resulted in increased sugar prices and the rapid expansion of beet sugar production in western Europe. It is estimated that by 1880 the total production of beet sugar, almost all of it in western Europe, equalled world cane sugar production.[9]

The expansion of sugar beet production in western Europe was the result of rising sugar prices, tariffs on imported sugar that had been designed for raising revenue but which provided substantial protection for beet sugar production, and by the payment of export bounties or subsidies by the European producer countries. By the end of the nineteenth century England imported mainly beet sugar, made relatively cheap by export bounties. The United States was also a major importer of beet sugar from Europe, with the expansion of such imports largely displacing Cuba from the U.S. market.[10]

One of the minor ironies of life and politics is that one of the early enactments after the adoption of the Constitution was the imposition of a tariff on sugar, in an act passed on 4 July 1789. Since no sugar was produced in the United States at that time, the objective of the tariff was to raise revenue—which was also the objective the recently vanquished British had in mind.[11]

We have had duties on sugar from that day forward. However, from 1890 to 1894 there was no duty on the importation of raw sugar. For those years the domestic producing industry was protected by a two cent per pound subsidy or bounty and the refining industry protected by a tariff of 0.5 cent per pound on refined sugar.[12]

The 1890 removal of the U.S. tariff on raw sugar had a major effect upon Hawaii. Under an 1876 treaty between the United States and the Kingdom of Hawaii, Hawaiian sugar entered the United States duty free, giving it ready access to a highly protected market. The Hawaiian sugar industry prospered, with output increasing from 13,000 tons in 1876 to 140,000 tons in 1890. In fact, sugar developed into the most important industry in Hawaii. After 1890 the "price of Hawaiian sugar fell sharply. Hawaiian sugar producers did not receive the bounty. General unrest followed leading to revolt against the monarchy of Queen Eiliuokalani in 1893 and the establishment of the Republic of Hawaii in 1894." [13]

The reimposition of the tariff in 1894 was done, at least in part, to protect Hawaiian sugar production. Hawaii became a part of the United States in 1898, apparently to prevent its exclusion from the protected U.S. market for sugar. And one must admit that, so far, the decision has had the desired result.[14]

Thus sugar policy has long been associated with controversy and conflict, with many economic, political and military implications. As a cause, alleged or real, for the American Revolution, with its development encouraged in inappropriate places by Napoleon as he set upon the military conquest of the whole of Europe, and as a a major factor in the overthrow of a queen and the impetus for the acquisition of territory that turned out to be our forty-ninth state, sugar is a topic with far broader implications than costs to consumers and taxpayers and benefits to producers. But it is primarily these latter consequences, and not the much more romantic and, perhaps, more important ramifications of sugar's role in history, that will be considered in this essay.

# CHAPTER II

# THE U.S. SUGAR PROGRAM

The present structure of our sugar policy was established by the Sugar Act of 1934, also known as the Jones-Costigan Act. On 8 February 1934 President Roosevelt sent a message to the Congress requesting action on sugar. A few sentences from that message appear particularly appropriate at this time when new sugar legislation will soon be under consideration:

> There is a school of thought which believes that sugar ought to be on the free list. This belief is based on the high cost of sugar to the American consuming public.
>
> The annual gross value of the sugar crop to American beet and cane growers is approximately $60,000,000. Those who believe in the free importation of sugar say that the 2 cents a pound tariff is levied mostly to protect this $60,000,000 crop and that it costs our consuming public every year more than $200,000,000 to afford this protection.
>
> I do not at this time recommend placing sugar on the free list. I feel that we ought first to try out a system of quotas with the three-fold objective of keeping down the price of sugar to consumers, of providing for the retention of beet and cane farming within our continental limits, and also to provide against further expansion of this necessarily expensive industry.[1]

Of the three objectives stated by President Roosevelt, it should be obvious that only one has been achieved, namely, the retention of sugar beet and cane farming within our continental limits. The program has not, on the average, kept down the cost of sugar to consumers nor has it prevented the "further expansion of this necessarily expensive industry." But more on these points later.

The U.S. sugar program is relatively simple. Its main features are:

1. yearly establishment by the secretary of agriculture of total annual U.S. consumption requirements;

2. allocation of total consumption requirements among domestic areas (cane and beet producing areas) and foreign countries;

3. establishment of import quotas to control shipments by foreign countries of both raw and refined sugar to the United States;

4. establishment of limits on quantities of direct-consumption sugar from Hawaii and Puerto Rico shipped to the continental United States;

5. benefit payments made to domestic producers (including producers in Puerto Rico) for abiding by the terms of the Sugar Act;

6. a tax of $0.50 per hundredweight of raw sugar on all sugar used in the United States;

7. a tariff of $0.625 per hundredweight of raw sugar; and

8. provisions for the "fair division of the benefits" of the sugar program.[2]

The effort to control the division of sugar program benefits has resulted in a variety of measures and regulations. A farmer, to be eligible to receive the benefit payments, called conditional payments, must pay workers a wage at least equal to the minimum wages established for his area by the secretary of agriculture, cannot employ children under the age of fourteen years, and if a grower is also a processor of cane or beets grown by others, that grower must pay prices at least equal to minimum prices as determined by the secretary of agriculture.

The receipt of conditional payments may also be contingent upon a producer abiding by an acreage allotment or, more accurately, a "proportionate share." When it is anticipated that a domestic area will supply more than its quota, the secretary of agriculture imposes marketing allotments on sugar processors and proportionate shares on sugar cane and beet growers in the area. In recent years, proportionate shares have been established for sugar cane production in Louisiana and Florida, but not in the beet areas, since the output of sugar beets has been less than the quota allocated to the beet producing areas. Proportionate shares have never been imposed in Hawaii, and they have not been used in Puerto Rico since 1956.

Conditional payments made to producers are graduated, declining as the amount of sugar produced on a farm increases. The payment is at the rate of $0.80 per hundredweight of raw sugar up to 350 short tons and declines to $0.30 per hundredweight for any output in excess of 30,000 tons. The absolute level of payment has

10

remained constant for three decades. In recent years these payments have been from 14 to 15 percent of the prices received for sugar beets and 11 to 12 percent of the prices received for mainland sugar cane. In addition, quite modest payments are made each year to compensate farmers for low yields or abandonment of fields due to natural causes, such as drought, flood, storms, freezing, disease, or insects.

The domestic price of sugar is determined through the establishment of the annual consumption requirement and the use of the available authority to limit total sugar marketings to approximately that figure. The annual consumption requirement, which may be adjusted from time to time within the year, is set to produce a price near the price objective defined in the October 1971 amendments to the Sugar Act of 1948:

> The price objective . . . is a price for raw sugar which would maintain the same ratio between such price and the average of the parity index (1967=100) and the wholesale price index (1967=100) as the ratio that existed between (1) the simple average of the monthly price objective calculated for the period September 1, 1970 through August 31, 1971 under this section as in effect immediately prior to the date of enactment of the Sugar Act Amendments of 1971, and (2) the simple average of such two indexes for the same period.[3]

The price objective for the period indicated was 8.55 cents per pound and very close to the actual price in 1971, namely, 8.52 cents. Stated simply, the price objective changes over time in the same percentage as the simple average of wholesale prices and the parity index, which is an index of prices paid by farmers for commodities and services, interest, taxes, and wage rates. Prior to 1971 a price objective, defined quite similarly, was defined in the legislation as a general guideline to the secretary of agriculture in determining and adjusting consumption requirements. In 1971 the Sugar Act was amended to require that

> the determination of requirements of consumers shall be adjusted to the extent necessary to attain such price objective whenever the simple average of prices of raw sugar for seven consecutive market days is 4 percentum or more (or in the case of any seven consecutive market day period ending after October 31 of any year and before March 1 of the following year, 3 percentum or more) above or below the average price objective so determined for the preceding two calendar months. . . .[4]

This is a requirement for really fine tuning, but the tools available are apparently adequate to the task. For example, during 1972 the monthly average spot price ranged from 3.3 percent below to 2.7 percent above the monthly price objective. Even in 1973, when agricultural and food prices generally rose by substantial percentages, the spot sugar prices stayed very close to the price objective.

## The Establishment of Quotas

In terms of competing interests, one of the most critical elements of the sugar program is the determination of quotas for the various producing areas. Quotas—rights to market sugar in the United States—are now established for four domestic areas and thirty-five foreign countries. Quotas are now reserved for two additional countries—Cuba and Southern Rhodesia.

The legislation allocates basic quotas distributing the right to market sugar among the contesting claimants. Prior to 1956, the main foreign suppliers were Cuba and the Philippines—together they provided 97 percent or more of all sugar imports. In 1962, after the cessation of imports from Cuba, the number of countries given quotas was increased to more than thirty. The 1971 amendments distribute quotas among the various areas according to a basic quota and temporary quotas, with the latter referring to the reserved quotas for Cuba and Southern Rhodesia as currently distributed among all other foreign quota holders.

In addition, the legislation provides for the reallocation of any deficits in the sugar supplied—the shortfall of actual deliveries below the quotas for one or more areas. The reallocation of deficits can be quite substantial. In 1972, for example, the combined deficit for the domestic beet sugar area and Hawaii and Puerto Rico was 1,049,600 tons.[5] All of this deficit was allocated to foreign countries.

The secretary of agriculture is required to periodically review the relationship between marketings of the domestic producing areas and imports from the countries that have sugar quotas. If he determines that a domestic area will not be able to meet its full quota, the deficit is to be allocated to foreign countries and not to other domestic areas.

The 1973 allocations of the two types of quotas are given in Table 1. This table was publicly announced on 31 October 1972. Note that the secretary of agriculture projected deficits for the domestic areas amounting to 794,333 short tons and that these deficits were allocated among the Philippines and Western Hemisphere countries as required by law. (Subsequently the deficit projection

# Table 1

## SUGAR QUOTAS AND PRORATIONS FOR 1973

| Production Area | Basic Quota | Temporary Quotas and Prorations Pursuant to Sec. 202(d) [a] | Deficits and Prorations | Total Quotas and Prorations |
|---|---|---|---|---|
| | | Short tons, raw value | | |
| Domestic beet sugar | 3,644,333 | | −144,333 | 3,500,000 |
| Mainland cane sugar | 1,625,667 | | | 1,625,667 |
| Texas cane area | 20,000 | | | 20,000 |
| Hawaii | 1,110,000 | | | 1,110,000 [b] |
| Puerto Rico | 855,000 | | −650,000 | 205,000 [b] |
| Total domestic areas | 7,255,000 | | −794,333 | 6,460,667 |
| Philippines | 1,126,020 | 11,803 | 238,935 | 1,376,758 [b] |
| Dominican Republic | 424,144 | 144,568 | 117,061 | 685,773 |
| Mexico | 375,103 | 127,851 | 103,525 | 606,479 |
| Brazil | 365,825 | 124,690 | 100,965 | 591,480 |
| Peru | 261,777 | 89,225 | 72,248 | 423,250 |
| West Indies | 136,521 | 46,532 | 37,679 | 220,732 |
| Ecuador | 54,012 | 18,409 | 14,907 | 87,328 |
| Argentina | 50,698 | 17,280 | 13,992 | 81,970 |
| Costa Rica | 45,728 | 15,586 | 12,621 | 73,935 |
| Colombia | 45,065 | 15,360 | 12,438 | 72,863 |
| Panama | 42,746 | 14,570 | 11,797 | 69,113 [b] |
| Nicaragua | 42,746 | 14,570 | 11,797 | 69,113 |
| Venezuela | 40,757 | 13,893 | 11,249 | 65,899 |
| Guatemala | 39,101 | 13,327 | 10,792 | 63,220 |
| El Salvador | 28,497 | 9,713 | 7,865 | 46,075 |
| British Honduras | 22,533 | 7,681 | 6,219 | 36,433 |
| Haiti | 20,544 | 7,002 | 5,670 | 33,216 |
| Honduras | 7,953 | 2,710 | 2,195 | 12,858 |
| Bolivia | 4,308 | 1,469 | 1,189 | 6,966 |
| Paraguay | 4,308 | 1,469 | 1,189 | 6,966 |
| Australia | 166,344 | 46,276 | | 212,620 |
| Republic of China | 69,255 | 19,266 | | 88,521 |
| India | 66,604 | 18,529 | | 85,133 |
| South Africa | 47,054 | 13,090 | | 60,144 |
| Fiji Islands | 36,450 | 10,141 | | 46,591 |
| Mauritius | 24,521 | 6,822 | | 31,343 |
| Swaziland | 24,521 | 6,822 | | 31,343 |
| Thailand | 15,243 | 4,240 | | 19,483 |
| Malawi | 12,260 | 3,410 | | 15,670 |
| Malagasy Republic | 9,941 | 2,766 | | 12,707 |
| Ireland | 5,351 | | | 5,351 [b] |
| Total foreign | 3,615,930 | 829,070 | 794,333 | 5,239,333 |
| Total | 10,870,930 | 829,070 | | 11,700,000 |

a Prorations of the quotas withheld from Cuba, Southern Rhodesia, Bahamas and Uganda.

b Direct-consumption limits in tons: Hawaii, 40,356; Puerto Rico, 169,000; Philippines, 59,920; Panama, 3,817; Ireland, 5,351.

**Source:** Agricultural Stabilization and Conservation Service, U.S. Department of Agriculture, *Sugar Reports,* no. 246 (November 1972), p. 6.

was reduced and new prorations were made, but these changes are not presented in the table.)

## Sugar Prices: United States and World Market

The purpose of all this regulation and machinery is to insulate the price of sugar in the United States from world market prices. And this objective has been achieved with great consistency. For example, in July 1972 the world price of raw sugar was 5.58 cents per pound; the domestic price, duty paid, in New York was 9.17 cents. In December 1972 the world price had increased to 9.08 cents and the price in New York was 9.19 cents. After including the estimated cost of freight, insurance, and unloading charges, and taking into account the tariff of 0.625 cents per pound, the exporter who shipped to the United States received 1.11 cents per pound less for sugar in December 1972 than could be obtained on the world market.

Why would an exporter sell sugar to the United States at a loss? The reason is that over the past twenty-five years sales of sugar to the United States have netted substantially more than sales on the world market. The extent of this advantage is discussed in Chapter III.

# CHAPTER III

# SUGAR SUPPLY AND TRADE

In this chapter we shall consider two aspects of sugar supply: the supply for the world and the supply for the United States. An estimate of the cost of the sugar program to U.S. consumers and taxpayers is quite directly related to supply conditions for sugar and the nature and extent of restrictions currently imposed upon international trade in sugar in the United States and most other industrial countries.

## Distribution of the World Production of Sugar

In 1971 the world production of sugar was 74 million metric tons, raw value. Of this, 42 percent was beet sugar and the remainder was cane sugar.

Table 2 shows the distribution of world sugar output in 1971 by major regions and by cane and beet sugar. It may come as a surprise that Europe produces more sugar than any other continent. In 1971 Europe produced slightly more than a third of the world's total. Almost all of the European sugar is beet sugar—more than 97 percent. In 1971 Europe produced somewhat more than four-fifths of the world's output of beet sugar, and about half of the remainder was produced in the United States, with most of the rest being produced in China and Japan.

The major producers of cane sugar are in Central America (15 percent of the world's sugar output) and South America (about 13 percent of world production). China, India, and the Philippines are also important producers.

There are very few industrial countries that do not produce some sugar. In Europe, only Norway and Luxembourg have resisted

## Table 2

### SUGAR PRODUCTION BY REGION AND TYPE, 1971 [a]

| Region | Cane | Beet | Total | Percent of World |
|---|---|---|---|---|
| | Million metric tons | | | |
| Europe | 0.4 | 25.4 | 25.8 | 34.8 |
| EEC | 0.4 | 8.3 | 8.7 | 11.7 |
| U.S.S.R. | — | 8.4 | 8.4 | 11.3 |
| United Kingdom | — | 1.1 | 1.1 | 1.5 |
| North America | 2.4 | 3.2 | 5.7 | 7.7 |
| United States | 2.4 | 3.1 | 5.6 | 7.6 |
| Canada | — | 0.1 | 0.1 | 0.1 |
| Central America | 11.3 | — | 11.3 | 15.3 |
| Cuba | 6.0 | — | 6.0 | 8.1 |
| Mexico | 2.5 | — | 2.5 | 3.4 |
| Dominican Republic | 1.1 | — | 1.1 | 1.5 |
| South America | 9.3 | 0.2 | 9.5 | 12.8 |
| Brazil | 5.3 | — | 5.3 | 7.2 |
| Paraguay | 0.9 | — | 0.9 | 1.2 |
| Colombia | 0.7 | — | 0.7 | 0.9 |
| Asia | 11.7 | 1.9 | 13.6 | 18.4 |
| China | 2.3 | 0.8 | 3.1 | 4.2 |
| Taiwan | 0.8 | — | 0.8 | 1.1 |
| India | 4.0 | — | 4.0 | 5.4 |
| Philippines | 2.2 | — | 2.2 | 3.0 |
| Japan | 0.3 | 0.4 | 0.7 | 0.9 |
| Indonesia | 0.8 | — | 0.8 | 1.1 |
| Thailand | 0.6 | — | 0.6 | 0.8 |
| Africa | 4.7 | 0.2 | 4.9 | 6.6 |
| South Africa | 1.7 | — | 1.7 | 2.3 |
| Egypt | 0.5 | — | 0.5 | 0.7 |
| Mauritius | 0.7 | — | 0.7 | 0.9 |
| Australia | 2.7 | — | 2.7 | 3.6 |
| Fiji | 0.4 | — | 0.4 | 0.5 |
| World | 43.0 | 31.0 | 74.0 | 100.0 |

[a] Sugar in terms of raw value.

**Note:** Countries listed are the major producers only. Regional totals are for *all* countries in each region.

**Source:** International Sugar Organization, *Sugar Year Book,* 1971 (London, 1972), pp. 298-305.

the opportunity. New Zealand also produces no sugar. Otherwise, often without regard to cost, the industrial countries have supported sugar production.

# World Trade in Sugar

In 1971 world trade in sugar was 21 million metric tons, approximately 30 percent of world production.[1] The total includes trade in both raw and refined sugar. In 1971 total world net imports amounted to 18 million metric tons since some countries both import and export sugar, with some of the exports consisting of refined imported raw sugar.

A 1968 study by K. A. Ingersent of the University of Nottingham indicated that 14.9 million metric tons of raw sugar were exported. Of this amount 8.75 million metric tons went to preferential markets under the U.S. sugar quotas, the British Commonwealth Sugar Agreement, and from Cuba to the U.S.S.R. and China. The 6.15 million ton remainder moved at what might be called world market prices. Thus, of the total trade in raw sugar, approximately 60 percent moved under special and restricted market arrangements.[2]

Table 3 provides data on world net imports of sugar by major regions and for individual important importing countries. The largest importers of sugar are the United States, with almost 30 percent of the total, Japan, with 14 percent, and the United Kingdom, with almost 12 percent. Together these three countries account for 56 percent of the world's net imports of sugar. Europe (excluding the United Kingdom) imports less than 9 percent of the total. While one may be critical of the U.S. sugar program, as I am, it should be noted that the U.S. provides the world's largest market for sugar imports and that we have been more restrained in expanding production to meet consumption than most other industrial countries.

## Sugar Prices Received by Producers

There are two levels of sugar prices that are of interest: the prices paid to producers for sugar cane and sugar beets, and the prices that consumers must pay at the retail store. On both scores one finds a great deal of regulation by governments. There are only a few net importing countries in which the consumer has access to sugar at prices that reflect the world prices for raw sugar.

Table 4 provides data on sugar prices for several countries. Some degree of consideration was given consumers in the United Kingdom, Canada, Switzerland, Iraq, and Norway. Japan and the Netherlands had the honor of imposing the highest prices on their consumers: in excess of sixteen cents per pound. The United States is in an intermediate position, having a retail price in 1969 that was approximately the average for the importing countries. But it should

**Table 3**

WORLD NET IMPORTS OF SUGAR BY REGIONS
AND CERTAIN COUNTRIES, 1971 [a]

| Region | Net Imports (million metric tons) | Percent of Total |
|---|---|---|
| Europe | 3.5 | 20.3 |
| EEC | −0.8 | −4.7 |
| United Kingdom | 2.0 | 11.6 |
| East Germany | 0.3 | 1.7 |
| Switzerland | 0.3 | 1.7 |
| U.S.S.R. | 0.1 | 0.6 |
| North America | 6.0 | 34.9 |
| United States | 5.1 | 29.7 |
| Canada | 0.9 | 5.2 |
| Central America | 0.0 | 0.0 |
| South America | 0.2 | 1.2 |
| Asia | 5.7 | 33.1 |
| Japan | 2.4 | 14.0 |
| South Vietnam | 0.3 | 1.7 |
| Ceylon | 0.4 | 2.3 |
| Burma | 0.3 | 1.7 |
| Africa | 1.6 | 9.3 |
| Algeria | 0.3 | 1.7 |
| Sudan | 0.2 | 1.2 |
| Morocco | 0.2 | 1.2 |
| Oceania | 0.2 | 1.2 |
| New Zealand | 0.2 | 1.2 |
| Total | 17.2 | 100.0 |

[a] Sugar, whether imported raw or refined, in terms of raw value.

**Note:** Countries listed are the major importers only. Regional totals are for *all* countries in each region.

**Source:** International Sugar Organization, *Sugar Year Book,* 1971, pp. 323-331.

be noted that the U.S. retail price from 1966 through 1969 was three cents or more above the Canadian retail price. In several of the net exporting countries consumers do not do all that well either. Such net exporters as France, India, Denmark, and Venezuela show rather little concern for their own consumers. (Though in 1969 the average retail price in the exporting countries of Brazil, Mexico, Cuba, Peru, and Colombia appear to be in line with world market prices.)

It is impossible in this limited space to fully reflect the numerous complexities that affect the comparability of prices received by

## Table 4

### RETAIL PRICE OF SUGAR FOR SELECTED NET IMPORTING AND EXPORTING COUNTRIES [a]

(U.S. cents per pound)

| | 1965 | 1966 | 1967 | 1968 | 1969 |
|---|---|---|---|---|---|
| **Net importing countries** | | | | | |
| United States | 11.6 | 11.8 | 12.2 | 12.2 | 12.2 |
| United Kingdom | 11.1 | 9.5 | 9.3 | 8.5 | 8.8 |
| Japan | 14.2 | 17.0 | 15.6 | 16.1 | 16.4 |
| West Germany | 14.0 | 13.9 | 14.0 | — | 13.7 |
| Canada | 8.8 | 8.8 | 8.1 | 8.9 | 8.8 |
| Netherlands | 14.0 | 14.4 | 14.7 | 15.6 | 16.8 |
| Spain | 11.8 | 11.8 | — | — | 10.8 |
| Iran | — | 14.4 | 14.4 | 13.8 | 14.0 |
| Pakistan | 18.0 | 17.2 | 13.9 | 17.9 | 17.3 |
| Egypt | — | — | — | 12.0 | 11.8 |
| Switzerland | 11.2 | 8.9 | 8.1 | 9.3 | 9.1 |
| Chile | — | — | — | 11.1 | 11.2 |
| Sweden | 15.0 | 12.7 | 13.6 | 13.0 | 13.0 |
| Iraq | 9.5 | 8.3 | 8.3 | 8.3 | 8.3 |
| Ceylon | 14.0 | 14.0 | 14.0 | 12.1 | 12.1 |
| Algeria | 11.4 | — | — | 14.7 | 15.2 |
| Ireland | 11.1 | 10.5 | 11.4 | — | 10.5 |
| Norway | 10.8 | 6.8 | 6.0 | 6.3 | 7.3 |
| Average price | 12.4 | 12.0 | 11.7 | 12.0 | 12.1 |
| **Net exporting countries** | | | | | |
| Brazil | 6.1 | 7.8 | 6.6 | 6.4 | — |
| India | — | 12.0 | 7.9 | 10.1 | 10.0 |
| France | 12.6 | 12.6 | 13.1 | — | — |
| Mexico | 5.6 | 5.6 | 5.6 | — | 5.6 |
| Italy | 16.0 | 17.4 | 17.1 | 17.1 | — |
| South Africa | 7.0 | 7.0 | 8.0 | — | 10.9 |
| Australia | 10.2 | 10.2 | 10.0 | 11.7 | 11.7 |
| Philippines | — | — | 8.1 | 7.9 | 9.6 |
| Turkey | — | 13.7 | 13.7 | 13.9 | 16.4 |
| Cuba | 7.0 | 6.9 | — | — | 6.9 |
| Yugoslavia | 13.3 | 9.5 | 9.5 | — | 9.7 |
| Colombia | 7.2 | — | — | 6.1 | 5.4 |
| Belgium | 13.9 | 14.4 | 16.7 | 15.5 | — |
| Venezuela | — | — | 10.1 | 10.1 | 10.2 |
| Peru | 5.8 | 6.1 | 6.1 | 6.7 | 5.8 |
| Austria | 11.9 | 11.9 | 11.9 | 11.9 | 12.0 |
| Denmark | 8.3 | 10.3 | 13.5 | — | 14.1 |
| China (Taiwan) | 13.4 | 10.8 | 13.2 | 11.5 | 13.0 |
| Average price | 9.9 | 10.4 | 10.5 | 10.5 | 9.9 |
| Average all countries | 11.2 | 11.2 | 11.1 | 11.2 | 11.1 |

[a] As of January 1 of the selected years.

**Note:** Consumption in these listed countries of 47,400,000 tons represents 62 percent of 1969 world consumption of 75,900,000 short tons, raw value. Prices in unlisted countries, some of which have centrally planned economies, are believed to average higher.

**Source:** International Sugar Organization annuals, as reprinted in U.S. House of Representatives, Committee on Agriculture, *The United States Sugar Program,* 91st Congress, 2d session, 31 December 1970, p. 9.

farmers for sugar. The sugar content of sugar cane, as well as of sugar beets, varies from country to country. In some cases, such as the United States, the prices received by farmers for cane or beets do not reflect the full return. Additional payments are made to producers, and these may or may not be reflected in published data. Thus the data provided here should be considered only as approximations, but they are accurate enough to reflect the wide range in returns to producers. I believe the errors in the data are small compared to the absolute differences in the levels of returns.

I have attempted in Table 5 to adjust prices received for sugar cane and sugar beets to a comparable basis. These two raw products differ in two important respects in terms of their value in the same market situation: sugar content and the cost of obtaining refined sugar from the raw material. Sugar beets have a higher sugar content than does sugar cane, and it is apparently somewhat cheaper to obtain refined sugar from sugar beets, at least in the United States. I have made the adjustment of the prices of sugar beets to the prices

## Table 5

### ESTIMATED PRICES RECEIVED BY SUGAR PRODUCERS, ADJUSTED TO SUGAR CANE PRICES, 1970

| Country and Kind | Prices Received, Sugar Cane Basis (dollars per metric ton) | Production (million tons, raw value) |
|---|---|---|
| Sugar cane | | |
| Mexico | 4.20 | 2.5 |
| Brazil | 4.45 | 5.0 |
| Taiwan | 5.70 | 0.7 |
| Mauritius [a] | 6.80 | 0.6 |
| Australia [a] | 10.50 | 2.2 |
| United States | 12.90 | 2.7 |
| Sugar beets [b] | | |
| France | 11.55 | 2.4 |
| Germany | 11.55 | 2.1 |
| Denmark | 11.55 | 0.3 |
| United Kingdom [a] | 11.55 | 1.1 |
| Netherlands | 12.22 | 0.7 |
| United States | 12.90 | 3.1 |

[a] Prices are for 1969.

[b] Actual sugar beet prices received were $17.00 for France, Germany, Denmark and the United Kingdom, $18.00 for the Netherlands and $19.00 for the United States. Payments are included for the United States and United Kingdom.

**Source:** Food and Agricultural Organization of the United Nations, *Production Yearbook,* 1971, pp. 552-555.

of sugar cane by using the price relationships that existed in the United States in 1970. In that year the farm price, including government payments, for sugar cane in the mainland producing areas was $12.90 per metric ton; the price of sugar beets was $19.00 per metric ton. Sugar beet prices have been reduced by 32 percent to obtain a more direct comparison with sugar cane prices. The actual sugar beet prices per ton are indicated in a footnote to Table 5. It should be recognized that the sugar content of both sugar cane and sugar beets varies from country to country and that these differences have not been taken into account.

Before commenting on the contents of Table 5, it should be noted that, if data were presented for some other year, the price relationships would differ somewhat. However, an examination of the price data in the United Nations Food and Agricultural Organization (FAO) source for a period of approximately fifteen years indicates that, except for two or three years between 1955 and 1970, the price relationships in Table 5 reflect the general pattern of national prices for that period. Further, as noted later, the lowest prices do not reflect what producers would have received if their output had all been sold at the world price.

The price data indicate that in 1970 Mexico and Brazil had producer prices that were only 40 percent of those received by producers in Western Europe and in the United States. Mexico and Brazil together produced a tenth of the world's sugar in 1970. Thus the low producer prices do not apply to insignificant levels of production. Nor has production stagnated. In 1971 sugar cane output in Brazil was 27 percent greater than in the years 1961-65 and 30 percent greater in Mexico.[3]

It is obvious that a great deal of sugar is being produced under high-cost conditions and, at least for the countries included in Table 5, *the United States has the highest costs.*

### Sugar Export Prices

As will be shown later (Table 6), the world market price for sugar is highly variable, though for most of the past two decades it has been substantially below the U.S. import price of raw sugar. In 1970 a country that shipped raw sugar to the United States received an average of 6.94 cents per pound. This was equal to the U.S. market price for raw sugar minus a tariff duty of 0.625 cents per pound and costs of transportation.[4] If, in the same year, the same country sold sugar at a comparable location in the world market, it received 3.75 cents per pound. Thus sugar shipped to the United States, for those countries with quotas, was worth 3.19 cents per pound more than the same product sold in the world market—the market that exists outside of preferential arrangements. This difference, which is called the quota premium, varies from year to year, reaching a high of 4.56 cents per pound in 1968—when the world market price of sugar was only 1.98 cents. In 1963 the premium was a negative 1.23 cents per pound since sugar sold to the world market brought more than sugar sold to the United States.

None of the important producers and exporters of sugar are entirely outside of some special arrangement. Thus the prices received by producers reflect an average of prices obtained from one or more preferential arrangement and the world market. A study of 1968 average export prices by K. A. Ingersent indicates that four exporters received an average price of less than $60 per metric ton while six received prices of $140 and more. During that year sugar exported to the United States had an f.o.b. value of about $145 per ton, while the U.S.S.R. paid Cuba a price of $135 per ton, and sugar sold under the Commonwealth Sugar Agreement varied in price from $103 to $112 per ton. The world price of raw sugar was $42 per ton.

The range in export prices was even wider than indicated by the foregoing distribution. The Ryukyu Islands had access to the high-priced Japanese market, and the average export price was approximately $200 per ton. South Africa, on the other hand, sold little sugar into preferential markets and had an average export price of about $55 per ton. Of the large exporters, the Philippines had the highest average price since all of her 1968 sugar exports went to the U.S. market, and a return of $145 per ton was realized. Mexico also had a relatively high export price of nearly $135 per ton since almost all of her sugar was exported to the United States. Brazil, which exports slightly under half of its sugar to the United States, had an average export value of approximately $100 per ton. The Dominican Republic also had a relatively high export price, just under $135 per ton.[5] It is hard to imagine that there is another market in which greater distortions exist.

## The U.S. Sugar Supply: 1925 to 1959

From 1925 through 1929 Cuba supplied from 47 to 58 percent of U.S. sugar consumption, with an average of 53 percent. Other foreign countries supplied less than 0.5 percent. The remaining supplies came from domestic areas, including the Philippines. The latter supplied about 8 percent, while Hawaii provided approximately 12 percent and Puerto Rico about 9 percent. The continental areas of the United States thus provided the remainder, or about 18 percent, and almost all of that was beet sugar (16 percent of total consumption).

With the increase in tariff duties in 1930 and the drop in world sugar prices with the onset of the Great Depression, Cuban production and exports fell. Cuban production was 5.8 million short tons of raw sugar in 1928-29 but only 2.2 million short tons in 1932-33. Cuban exports to the U.S. were 4.2 million short tons in 1929 but only 1.8 million short tons in 1932 and somewhat less in 1933.[6] The price of raw sugar in Cuba declined 56 percent from 1929 to 1932.[7] In 1932 the New York wholesale price of raw sugar was 2.9 cents per pound, and the duty on Cuban sugar was 2.0 cents per pound.[8] Obviously, after paying the costs of transportation and the cost of extracting raw sugar from cane, there was little left as return for producing sugar cane.

The above facts are recited because they are relevant to the establishment of sugar quotas in the first sugar act. The Sugar Act of 1934 permitted the secretary of agriculture to determine the quotas on the basis of any three years during the period 1925-1933 that he considered to be the "most important representative three years." The law also specified that the quota for the mainland sugar beet area should be not less than 1,550,000 short tons, more than had ever been produced, and the quota for the mainland cane area not less than 260,000 short tons. The period selected for the U.S. offshore areas—except Hawaii—was 1931-33. For Hawaii the period was 1930-32.[9] After these determinations were made and the total consumption requirements were established, almost all the residual was allocated to Cuba. This residual was nearly equal to Cuban sugar exports to the United States in 1931-33. The quota established was 35 percent less than the average imports from Cuba for the 1925-33 period.

Thus one of the first effects of the sugar program was to hold sugar imports substantially below what they would have been if there were a moderate tariff (one of less than 50 percent) or free trade. Subsequent changes in the sugar program in 1937, 1948, 1951, and 1956 did not significantly change this general pattern. Two minor changes did occur. The share of the mainland cane area in the total quota was increased from 4.0 percent in 1934 to 6.3 percent in 1937. This increase occurred at the expense of the domestic beet area, Cuba, and Puerto Rico. The other change that occurred resulted from the fixing in the Philippine Trade Act of 1946 of an absolute quota for the Philippines of 980,000 short tons of raw sugar.

By 1959 the Philippines's share of the basic quotas had declined to 10.4 percent, down from 15.7 percent in the 1934 act. Prior to 1960 other changes in relative shares were not significant.[10]

During the period from 1934 to 1959 total shipments of sugar under the quotas increased from 6.6 million short tons to 9.2 million. Thus deliveries from all areas increased significantly during the period.[11]

## The U.S. Sugar Supply: 1960 to 1973

In 1959 Cuba supplied almost 35 percent of the U.S. sugar consumption. After the Castro revolution in Cuba, the Sugar Act was hurriedly amended, and in July 1960, the President was empowered to determine the Cuban sugar quota for the remainder of 1960 and the first three months of 1961. The quota was set at zero for the remainder of 1960, except for sugar already certified for entry into the United States. These actions meant that the United States had to find other sources that would provide approximately 3.2 million short tons of sugar for 1961.

The cessation of imports from Cuba served as a basis for a significant increase in quotas allocated to domestic areas. In 1959, if the consumption requirement had been 9.7 million short tons, the domestic area quotas would have been 53.5 percent of the total. In 1962 the domestic areas were given 59.9 percent of the total quotas, and in 1965, when the consumption requirement was 10.4 million short tons, their share was increased to 61.4 percent. Under the 1956 legislation, when consumption requirements exceeded a specified level, the domestic areas received quotas for 55 percent of the additional amounts. In 1962 the domestic areas were given 65 percent of the excess of consumption over a specified level.[12]

The 1962 act provided for establishing new producing areas for sugar beets. Six new processing plants were approved by the secretary of agriculture to serve 157,000 acres of sugar beets. Expanded facilities were approved for three other areas involving 14,600 acres. The total reserve or additional area amounted to almost 14 percent of the total area planted to sugar beets in 1966.[13]

The 1962 legislation did not provide for the specific allocation of the quota that was withheld from Cuba, though about 800,000 tons were assigned to specific countries. While special preference was to be given to countries in the Western Hemisphere, nearly 3 million tons of sugar could be shipped to the United States by any country that was a net exporter of sugar. A unique feature of the legislation was a variable levy on sugar, a rather interesting approach at a time when

24

the United States was so roundly condemning the European Economic Community for the use of the same device. The levy was authorized for three years (through 1964). The fee for quota sugar was set at 10 percent of the excess of the domestic price of raw sugar over the world price for 1962, at 20 percent for 1963, and at 30 percent for 1964. The levy for sugar brought in under the global quota was 100 percent of the difference. The fee was imposed only during 1962 since the world sugar price in 1963 and 1964 was equal to or greater than the U.S. price.

In 1965 the secretary of agriculture assigned quotas within the global quota to specific countries, based on the imports from such countries in 1963 and 1964. Imports in 1963 were given a weight of one and those for 1964 a weight of two.[14]

The Sugar Act amendments of 1965 were primarily concerned with the allocation of the sugar quota withheld from Cuba. The basic quotas for domestic areas were essentially the same in 1966 as in 1965. The Philippines did not get an increase in the basic quota, but was assigned 10.86 percent of any increase in consumption requirements above 9,700,000 tons. The quota for Cuba was set at 50 percent of the total amount assigned to foreign countries other than the Philippines. This quota was withheld and prorated among foreign countries other than the Philippines.

It is not clear to me, at least, how the quotas to foreign countries other than the Philippines were assigned. In 1959 only three countries other than Cuba and the Philippines had basic quotas in excess of 50,000 short tons. The total assigned to all "other countries" was 279,000 tons.[15] The amendments passed in 1965 assigned foreign quotas (other than to the Philippines) in excess of 3,000,000 tons to approximately thirty countries. Most, though not all, of the countries receiving quotas for 1966 had sold sugar to the United States between 1961 and 1965. The Special Subcommittee on Sugar of the House Committee on Agriculture issued an eight-page statement with the title *The Development of Foreign Sugar Quotas in H.R. 11135.* The report noted that there had been a search for a mathematical formula, and that the Department of Agriculture had worked out more than thirty different formulas based on sugar shipments to the United States for some or all of the years from 1961 through 1964. These results were rejected by the subcommittee. The subcommittee then specified nine criteria that they used in assigning quotas. But the criteria were so general that the numerous allocations would have been equally consistent. For example, two of the criteria were: "stability of supply—including the element of stability of the local government," and "the economic need of the country for a U.S. quota and the relative value of a quota to such country." [16] The distribution of the adjusted quotas—the basic quotas plus the distribution of the quotas withheld from Cuba and Southern Rhodesia —were allocated 58 percent to the Western Hemisphere, 29 percent to the Philippines, and 13 percent to all other countries.

The most recent change in sugar legislation occurred in 1971. The share of the domestic areas was left unchanged at between 61 and 62 percent when total requirements were 11.2 million short tons, with 65 percent of any increase in requirements being allocated to the domestic areas. However, significantly larger quotas were given to the mainland cane and beet areas and to Hawaii by reducing the quota for Puerto Rico by 285,000 tons. Puerto Rico had not fulfilled its quota for many years, and it is unlikely that Puerto Rican interests were affected by the change. However, the reallocation of the domestic quotas meant that a further inducement was given to production in other domestic areas.

The 1971 amendments authorized the secretary of agriculture to make allocations of acreage in both cane and beet areas for new or expanded facilities up to a total sufficient to provide for 200,000 short tons of raw sugar. Thus, the shift in allocations to the mainland and Hawaiian areas, combined with the establishment of new producing areas or enlargement of existing ones, meant that the potential for imports was reduced. Previously all of the shortfall in Puerto Rican deliveries had been allocated to the Philippines and Western Hemisphere countries. As production in domestic areas other than Puerto Rico expands, there will be smaller amounts to allocate to foreign quota holders.

The changes in the actual quotas for foreign countries were relatively modest in 1971. The sugar quota for Cuba, which had been withheld since 1961, was cut approximately in half. The basic quota for the Dominican Republic, which had been approximately the same as for Mexico and Brazil, was increased so that it was 50,000 short tons more than Brazil's and 60,000 short tons more than Mexico's. The administration had recommended that there be no relative change in the allocation of quotas among foreign countries.[17]

### Expansion of Sugar Production in the Western Hemisphere

One of the arguments made for the expansion of sugar production in domestic areas was to assure adequate supplies after the severing of diplomatic relations with Cuba. As indicated earlier, Cuba had supplied approximately 35 percent of the U.S. sugar supply in 1959. In the period 1955-59, before the U.S. market was open to Central and South American countries, sugar production in the Western Hemisphere outside of Canada, the United States, and Cuba averaged 8,129,000 short tons (raw value) annually. In the period 1960-64 production increased to 10,393,000 short tons, by 1966 it was 12.4 million short tons, and by 1972, 15.8 million tons.[18]

From the period 1955-59 through 1972 the increase in U.S. consumption and the reduction of imports from Cuba totaled 6.1 million tons, of which 3.1 million tons represented the reduction in imports from Cuba. Average annual production in domestic areas increased from 4,570,000 short tons in the period 1955-59 to 6,300,000 tons in 1972. However, the change in domestic production masks a sharp reduction in average annual production in Puerto Rico, from about 900,000 tons in 1955-59 to 150,000 tons in 1972.[19]

# CHAPTER IV

# THE PROTECTION OF SUGAR REFINING

The U.S. sugar program is generally considered to be a program to maintain a significant level of production of sugar cane and sugar beets in this country. In recent years the program has resulted in approximately 60 percent of total sugar supplies being provided by domestic production.

It is not generally understood, however, that the most protective and arbitrary features of the sugar program are the virtual prohibition of the importation of refined sugar into the United States and the strict limitation on the amount of sugar that can be refined in Hawaii and Puerto Rico. To be technically correct, I should refer to direct-consumption sugar rather than refined sugar, since the importation and marketing restraints apply to some forms of sugar other than refined sugar. Some sugar is used in food processing, when it is not fully refined, and some sugar is used in the form of syrup. All such forms of sugar, as well as refined sugar, are controlled, presumably because such types of sugar compete directly with refined sugar.

The sugar legislation that President Roosevelt proposed to Congress in 1934 would have given the secretary of agriculture discretionary authority to control the importation and movement of direct-consumption sugar, but it did not provide mandatory quotas. Such quotas were added in Congress after the strong urging of sugar refining interests. Ellsworth Bunker, then vice president of the National Refining Company, testified on 22 February 1934 "on behalf of the cane sugar refiners of the continental United States." His opening remarks are worth quoting:

> When an industry speaks in its own behalf, there is likely to be a suspicion that it has a hidden purpose or asks more than it is entitled to.
> That is emphatically not the case in this instance.

29

The sugar refining industry of the United States is appearing here for the frank purpose of asking only for its just dues.[1]

In his statement he argued that the U.S. mainland cane sugar refining industry was threatened with extinction because of the rapid increase in the importation of refined sugar between 1925 and 1933, when such imports increased from 20,000 tons to 700,000 tons. He argued that if other branches of the sugar industry were to be protected, then the refining industry merited similar consideration.

In the House hearings of 1934 the only voice raised against the inclusion of import restrictions on direct-consumption sugar was that of the Hershey Company, which produced and refined sugar in Cuba and shipped the refined sugar to the United States.[2]

The claim of the domestic refining industry for protection was based on a modest change in the differential in the tariff rate on raw and refined sugar that was made in the Smoot-Hawley Tariff Act of 1930. From 1922 through 1929 the tariff rate, per pound, on refined sugar had been 1.083 times the tariff rate on raw sugar. Under the Smoot-Hawley tariff the rate on refined sugar was 1.06 times that on raw sugar. It requires 1.07 tons of raw sugar to make a ton of refined sugar. The actual reduction in the nominal tariff for the refining amounted to one-fiftieth of a cent.

It is highly doubtful that the small change in the tariff structure was responsible for the sizable increase in the importation of refined sugar. The change in the competitive position of the U.S. cane sugar refining industry started before the change in the tariff rate. In 1925 refined sugar exports from the U.S. amounted to 326,000 tons; by 1930 such exports had declined to 77,000 tons.[3] Over the same five-year period imports of refined sugar from Cuba increased from 25,000 tons to 303,000 tons. The change in the tariff rate occurred on 18 June 1930. Cuban imports of refined sugar in 1929 were 270,000 tons.[4]

It seems safe to say that the U.S. cane sugar refining industry, which had not had any significant tariff protection since 1913, lost its ability to compete on a free trade basis toward the end of the 1920s. The search for protection was thus not altogether unexpected.

An interesting, and probably unique, aspect of the import quotas imposed on direct-consumption sugar in the 1934 act was that such quotas were applied to the U.S. territories—Hawaii, Puerto Rico, the Philippines, and the Virgin Islands—as well as to foreign countries. Thus it was not an act to protect the U.S. sugar refining industry, but only that part of the sugar refining industry located on the mainland. So far as I know, the constitutionality of this restraint on trade has never been challenged. *The restraint still applies to Hawaii as a state.*

30

The import quotas on refined sugar were *not* necessary to maintain the refining industry that processed sugar produced on the mainland. Sugar beet refining is a one step process in the sense that raw sugar is not produced as an intermediate product. And there was no possibility that the raw sugar produced from the cane of Louisiana and Florida would be exported to be refined and then shipped back to the United States. If the refineries that process domestically produced sugar are high cost relative to foreign refineries, the extra costs would be borne by farmers and consumers. But that fact, if it is a fact, was changed not at all by the import quota on refined sugar. Thus it was the sugar refining industry that processed raw sugar brought to the mainland, whether from U.S. territories or foreign countries, that was protected by the quotas on direct-consumption sugar.

The raw value refined sugar quotas for 1934 were (in tons):[5]

| | |
|---|---|
| Cuba | 418,385 |
| Philippines | 79,661 |
| Hawaii | 26,023 |
| Puerto Rico | 133,119 |
| Virgin Islands | 0 |

The Cuban refined sugar quota was set at 22 percent of its sugar quota, while the quotas for the Philippines, Hawaii, and Puerto Rico were set at the largest amounts shipped in any one of the years 1931, 1932, or 1933. In 1932 Cuba had shipped 471,000 tons as refined sugar, approximately 500,000 tons in terms of raw equivalent. The Cuban quota for refined sugar was some 40,000 tons (raw equivalent) less than its average shipments for the three-year period.

In 1937 there was greater opposition to the quotas on refined sugar. A lobbyist for Puerto Rico testifying at Senate hearings after the House had passed a sugar bill which was essentially unchanged from the 1934 act, said: "the real question [raised by refined sugar import quotas] is . . . whether American citizens on American soil just because they are not on the mainland can be subject to discriminatory legislation."[6] The answer then, as now, was obviously yes.

Ernest Gruening, director, Division of Territories and Island Possessions, Department of the Interior, also testified against the direct-consumption quotas as applied to the territories:

We feel that to impose this restriction is setting an inexcusable precedent, that it penalizes those areas of the United States which have no vote in the Congress, which have not even a voice in the Senate, which have a voice in the House but no vote, and that this in effect is the establishment of Old World colonialism, under the Stars and Stripes, something which should be repugnant and repulsive to our ideas of democracy.[7]

Even this rhetoric had no effect.

While efforts were made to reduce the quota for direct-consumption sugar, such efforts were unsuccessful until 1962. In the first major revision of the sugar legislation following the break in diplomatic relations with Cuba and the embargo on Cuban sugar exports to the United States, the direct-consumption quota was reduced from about 600,000 tons to 236,000 tons by the Sugar Act of 1962. Since the direct-consumption quotas are related to the overall sugar quota for the five countries or areas, the quotas totaled 277,000 tons in 1973.[8]

Sugar refining is an activity that can be carried out in developing countries, where almost all of the cane sugar is produced. Our sugar import policy is a significant barrier against such a development since we import nearly a quarter of all the sugar that moves in international trade. As a recent report prepared in the U.S. Department of Agriculture states, "In an age which stresses the need of developing countries to industrialize, it seems outdated to deny the opportunity of manufacturing refined sugar for exportation to developing countries by virtual embargo." [9]

I should note that most sugar in world trade moves as raw sugar because the production of refined sugar is so heavily protected. But this is not a rational argument for our protectionism.

I have made no effort to determine whether the U.S. cane sugar refining industry is competitive with foreign refining. Whether our cane refining is competitive or not is irrelevant. If it is competitive, the import quotas on direct-consumption sugar are unnecessary for its survival as a productive activity. If it is not competitive, then there is no national advantage served by maintaining it with an unknown degree of protection.

There is not even a significant employment argument for maintaining a high-cost cane sugar refining industry. In 1970, according to U.S. Department of Agriculture estimates, total employment amounted to 25 million hours or about 12,500 workers.[10] Part of this employment—about one quarter—is involved in processing domestically produced raw sugar. If the refiners' estimated margin—the difference between the price of raw sugar (duty paid) and the New York wholesale price—is too high by just twenty-five cents per hundredweight or $5.00 per short ton, the annual cost to consumers is $25 million or approximately a quarter of total wage and salary earnings in cane sugar refining in 1970.[11]

CHAPTER V

# AN EVIL SYSTEM

It is my normal practice to eschew pejorative words or phrases. And I gave considerable thought to the title of this short chapter. But the more I studied the congressional hearings on the sugar program and the many administrative decisions required to operate the program, the more convinced I became that the sugar program with its quotas and the processes by which those quotas are determined is truly an evil system. The quotas are valuable assets. Thus it is not surprising that great efforts are made to influence those who make the decisions with respect to the size of the quotas.

One evidence of the efforts made to obtain quotas is the list of witnesses at all congressional hearings dealing with the sugar program. The majority of the witnesses are paid lobbyists for foreign governments.

I have made no investigation of the role or influence of lobbyists. But a statement made by Senator Russell B. Long (D.-La.), chairman of the Senate Committee on Finance, and some of the further discussion on 18 June 1971 raise certain questions about the process:

THE CHAIRMAN: You made reference to the Argentine situation. My understanding was that when we acted on this thing in 1965, starting over on the House side, while everyone else hired a lobbyist to work for them, Argentina felt that it was not appropriate to send someone to appear before the committees of the Congress, with the result that on the House side they were granted a very small quota despite their help in our 1963-64 sugar crisis. On the Senate side, we restored the quota for them recommended by the Administration. But by the time we compromised it in conference, Argentina was treated very badly. It seems to me

33

almost simple justice that we ought to try to do better by Argentina than we did because they were treated so badly before. I wonder what your reaction is.

I might say those who hired lobbyists generally did very well. Argentina did not hire a lobbyist and just got the worst of it in all respects. That does not seem right to me, at least. . . .

What do you think would have been fair for Argentina in 1965 and what did they wind up with?

MR. MURPHY: Mr. Chairman, the administration recommended a quota of 63,684 tons at the then level of requirements. Argentina wound up with a quota at that level of 42,000 tons.

THE CHAIRMAN: As I recall it, the Finance Committee put in the figure you recommended and that was cut to 42, so they wound up with about 21,000 below where you thought they ought to be and where we thought they ought to be.

MR. MURPHY: That is right, Senator.

THE CHAIRMAN: Through no fault of ours, that would indicate that it is a good idea for somebody to hire a lobbyist, but we did not feel it ought to be that way on this committee. We felt they ought to be treated fairly whether they have a lobbyist or not.[1]

In 1970 the list of lobbyists for foreign governments was a long one. Small countries with very small quotas awarded in 1965, and with little prospects of obtaining larger quotas, felt it necessary to pay lobbyists to represent their interests. Examples of such countries are Mauritius and Swaziland, the former with a population of 800,000 and the latter with 400,000. Mauritius shipped about 19,000 tons of sugar to the U.S. in 1970 and Swaziland about 7,500 tons.[2] Both received substantially larger quotas in 1971, though obviously this cannot be attributed just to the employment of a lobbyist, for every other interested party had one too. The Fiji Islands, with a population of about 500,000, had a lobbyist, and three high officials of its government attended the House hearings.[3]

Having a lobbyist is not always enough. In 1971 Liberia, a country with close historical ties to the United States, found it necessary to be represented by the Honorable Harold D. Cooley, a member of Congress for more than three decades, chairman of the House Agriculture Committee for a dozen years, and a powerful force in shaping U.S. sugar legislation. Mr. Cooley appeared before the House Committee on Agriculture and the Senate Committee on

Finance. As indicated by the following quotation from the Senate hearings, he had no success at the House hearings:

> I indulge the hope that what I say before this committee will have more effect than what I said before the House Committee on Agriculture. Both the chairman and the ranking member of that committee are "hard of hearing," and sometimes they are both just naturally hard-headed. For many years the present chairman sat on my right, and I could speak into his good ear on the left. As strange as it may seem, when I came to testify, the chairman "turned over the chair" to some new member—and the chairman turned his wrong ear to me. I am not certain whether the ranking member turned his bad ear to me, or whether he just took out his hearing aid. The fact remains, however, what I said didn't go in—it went over their heads. They are both long-time friends of mine and are distinguished and dedicated public servants. I shall, of course, forgive them. I am glad that none of you gentlemen are wearing hearing aids, and I hope that you will hear some of the things I say.[4]

The senators either did not hear what Cooley was saying or they paid no attention: Liberia did not get a sugar quota.

There is no rational basis for establishing the allocation of any import quota for sugar, or anything else, among the competing interests. For a short period of time, it may make a little sense to base such quotas on recent imports for foreign countries and recent production levels for domestic areas. But over time many things change. The mainland cane area now has a quota five times that of 1934, the sugar beet area double that of 1934. The quota for the Philippines is only 40 percent larger now than in 1934. Cuba, of course, can now ship no sugar to the United States, though in 1934 it supplied nearly a third of total U.S. consumption.

It is understandable that foreign countries will invest significant sums in acquiring an asset as valuable as an import quota. It is also understandable that those who must decide how this asset is to be distributed will be influenced by many factors. There is no need to imply or infer corruption, but a decision that has little or no rational base must be made by *some* criterion, be it friendship, favor, or dislike. The basic difficulty is not with the individuals who must operate in this setting, but in the system itself. There is no escape.

### The Appearance of Evil

The operation of the sugar program is sufficiently complicated that it is easy for the uninitiated to be misled into an inference of corruption and favoritism where none exists. Such was the case with Jack Anderson, the nationally syndicated columnist. In an 11 October 1973 *Chicago Daily News* article, Anderson attempted to build a connection between a visit made by F. Donald Nixon, President Nixon's brother, to the Dominican Republic and an increase in the sugar quota of the Dominican Republic in 1970. It was claimed that Dominican President Juan Balaguer said that the Dominican Republic needed a larger sugar quota and that Donald Nixon received certain important concessions from him. Without any proof of a connection, Anderson wrote: "The following year, the Dominican sugar quota was increased from 458,000 to 515,000 tons."

There was no connection between Nixon's visit and the quota increase. The increase given to the Dominican Republic was what was called for by already existing legislation, and all countries in the Western Hemisphere received the same percentage increase in their "final basic quotas." For example, Brazil received an identical increase in its final basic quota. Anderson simply did not know what he was writing about.

Further, the final basic quota does not determine how much can be exported to the United States. That is determined by the "final adjusted quotas" which reflect the final basic quotas as modified by quota deficits and the proration of those deficits. Thus, the Dominican Republic shipped *less* sugar to the United States in 1970 than in 1969—678,209 tons compared to 693,068 tons. No other country in the Western Hemisphere suffered as large a percentage decline.[5]

It is true that the President had special authority to favor the Dominican Republic. Under the 1965 amendments to the Sugar Act he was permitted, if he deemed that the national interest would be served, to

> allocate any deficit to one or more countries with a quota on such basis as he finds appropriate, except for any deficit allocation to which the Republic of the Philippines is entitled and can fill. Acting under this provision of the Sugar Act, the President provided special allocations to the Dominican Republic of 123,000 tons in 1966, 105,000 tons in 1967, 75,000 tons in 1968, 50,000 tons in 1969, and 40,000 tons in 1970.[6]

Thus rather than favoring the Dominican Republic, the President *reduced* that part of the quota over which he had discretionary authority.

If Anderson had really been seeking light about the operation of the sugar program, he might have inquired how the Dominican Republic acquired a significant increase in its basic quota in the 1971 amendments to the Sugar Act. The increase was almost 61,000 tons in 1972 over 1971, while our two other largest suppliers—Mexico and Brazil—received reductions of about 16,000 tons each. The administration had recommended that only minor changes in the foreign quotas be made, namely, that minimum quotas be increased to 15,000 tons. In the Senate hearings, Julius L. Katz, deputy assistant secretary of state for international resources and food policy, objected to the significant changes in quotas made in the House bill.[7] I should hasten to add that the House bill did not favor the Dominican Republic. The changes that favored the Dominican Republic were apparently made in the Senate and accepted by the House in conference.[8]

It is perhaps unfair to be critical of the sugar program because of the inadequacies of Anderson's investigative machinery. Yet the program is so complicated that very few understand how it works. And in a system in which there is no rational basis for deciding whether Brazil or Mexico or Peru or some other country should have an increase in its quota, it is easy to suspect that favoritism had some role to play.

## Quotas on the Importation of Candy

Under the amendments of the Sugar Act of 1948 passed in 1971 the secretary of agriculture was required to impose quotas on the importation of sweetened chocolate, candy, and confectionery. The sum of the quotas was to be the larger of the imports for the average of three preceding years or 5 percent of U.S. consumption in the most recent year for which data were available.

This amendment was part of a section of the act that gave discretionary authority to the secretary of agriculture to impose quotas on sugar-containing products or mixtures if such products "will substantially interfere with the attainment of this Act." However, the limitations on the importation of candy was not discretionary, but required by the act.[9]

The import quotas on candy are not required to eliminate interference with the purposes of the Sugar Act. In 1971 the total weight of candy imported was about 70,000 tons.[10] At most, this candy contained 40,000 tons of sugar. During 1971 the total use of sugar in the U.S. was 11,288,000 tons. Thus the sugar contained in imported candy amounted to 0.0035 percent of the amount of sugar used in the United States—hardly enough to threaten the price structure that the Sugar Act was designed to achieve and protect.[11]

37

According to the Senate hearings in 1971, the inclusion of the quota on candy imports was designed not primarily to protect sugar, but to protect the candy industry.[12] It is of little moment that the global quota on candy imports has been larger than the actual imports of candy and that imports have not been restricted. But a wide variety of food products include sugar, and the Sugar Act could just as readily be used as the vehicle for limiting imports of products in addition to candy.

## Import Quotas and Our Trade Policy

One of the important objectives of our international trade policy for the past four decades has been the elimination of quantitative restrictions on international trade. The General Agreement on Tariffs and Trade (GATT) does provide for exceptions to the general rule that only tariffs should be used to regulate international trade in the case of agricultural products when a domestic program limits the output of a product. It would be exceedingly difficult for us to argue that we have effectively limited the domestic output of sugar. Since the sugar program was inaugurated in 1934 domestic sugar output has approximately doubled. Since 1947, when GATT was promulgated, our domestic sugar output has been increased by half. It is clear that the United States has not made a concerted effort to limit sugar production in a manner consistent with the spirit of the GATT exceptions permitting the use of quantitative restrictions—or, if the sugar program has been consistent with the GATT exception, the exception is meaningless as a limitation on the behavior of any government.

## The Sugar Program Is Different

An indication of both the arrogance and the political power of the large farms and firms that produce sugar could not have been more convincingly proven than by the following clause included in the 1971 amendments to the Sugar Act of 1948: "Sec. 412. The powers vested in the Secretary under this act shall terminate on December 31, 1974, or on March 31 of the year of termination of the tax imposed by section 4501 (a) of the Internal Revenue Code of 1954, whichever is the earlier date. . . ."

The tax referred to is the excise tax on sugar. This section appears to be innocuous enough until one consults Section 4501(b) of the Internal Revenue Code of 1934, Chapter 37, which says:

"Termination of Tax. No tax shall be imposed under this subchapter on the manufacture or use of sugar or articles composed in chief value of sugar after June 30, 1975, or June 30 of the first year commencing after the effective date of any law limiting payments under Title III of the Sugar Act of 1948, as amended, whichever is the earlier date."

The Agricultural Act of 1970 has imposed a $55,000 limit on payments to any one farmer under each of the major farm programs —wheat, cotton, and feed grains. The sixty-five large producers who in 1969 received payments of $55,000 or more apparently convinced Congress that a payment limitation was so serious that the Sugar Act should be terminated if such a limitation were imposed. It is rather obvious the large producers felt that it would not be possible to pass a payment limitation if the price of that limitation were the termination of the act—the 20,000 smaller producers would see that the act was maintained.

Data introduced at the 1971 House hearings by Representative Paul Findley (R.-Ill.) indicate the reason for the anxiety of the sixty-five large producers. These producers received a total of $15.5 million in 1961, including two payments of over one million dollars.[13] This was a sixth of all the payments made under the sugar program in that year. An approximate calculation indicates that these sixty-five farms (firms) produced about a quarter of the sugar output of the United States in 1969.[14] They received a smaller fraction of the payments because the rate of payment is lower for large farms than small farms.

# CHAPTER VI

# COSTS OF THE U.S. SUGAR PROGRAM

In this chapter I shall consider the costs of the U.S. sugar program to U.S. consumers and taxpayers. In Chapter VII I shall discuss the gains from the sugar program for U.S. farmers, farm workers, sugar refiners, and foreign producers of sugar.

There is no simple answer to the question: How much does the U.S. sugar program cost? An upper limit of the estimated cost can be arrived at by figuring the difference between the prices received by foreign producers for sales to the United States and to the world market and adjusting this result for the tariff, the excise tax on sugar, and the payments made to domestic sugar producers. Such an estimate is an upper limit because it implicitly assumes that if the United States removed all or most of the restraints on sugar imports that the world price of sugar would remain unchanged. In addition, it would make a difference whether the other industrial nations eliminated all or part of their restraints upon the importation of sugar since the world price would be affected by such actions.

### Elements of the Program's Cost

The cost of the sugar program to U.S. consumers and taxpayers consists of several elements: (1) the difference between the U.S. duty-free price of raw sugar and what the price of sugar would be if there were no sugar program, (2) a tariff of 0.625 cents per pound on all raw sugar imported, (3) an excise tax of 0.5 cents per pound on all raw sugar refined in the United States, and (4) benefit payments to domestic producers of sugar.

41

The first three cost components represent costs to consumers. However, the second and third provide revenue to the government and thus represent a benefit to taxpayers, assuming a constant size of federal government expenditures. The fourth component—the benefit payment to producers—represents a cost to taxpayers, but the payments have been less than the taxes (excise tax and import duties) collected, so there has been a net benefit to the taxpayers from the program.

In the following sugar program cost estimates, it is assumed that the alternative to the current sugar program is free trade in sugar by the United States and all other industrial countries. Obviously there are a number of other alternatives that could be considered. One such program might be a return to a modest level of tariff protection for both raw and refined sugar. Another might be to permit the free importation of sugar but to make deficiency payments to domestic producers in order to maintain sugar production at some specified level or percentage of U.S. consumption. These alternatives will not be considered in this chapter, but in Chapter VIII I shall consider some of the important implications of such alternatives.

It should also be noted that the sugar program cost estimates are the gross money costs. In effect what is being estimated are the gross income transfers, measured in money terms, from consumers and taxpayers to sugar producers, both domestic and foreign. The welfare costs—the losses in consumer welfare and excess production costs—are not measured. No account is taken of the fact that a lower domestic price of sugar would result in increased consumption. Since the price elasticity of demand for sugar in the United States is quite small, about $-0.2$,[1] the loss of consumer surplus due to the current program is much smaller than the income transfers involved. If the decline in the retail price of sugar were from fourteen cents to eleven cents per pound, and the consumption level prior to the price reduction were 11.4 million short tons, the value of the increase in consumers' surplus would be $15 million. As will be seen later, this is a relatively small part of the total cost to consumers.

### The Quota Premium

The quota premium is defined as the difference between the return from raw sugar sold to the United States and raw sugar sold to the world market, with the difference calculated for sugar f.o.b. in greater-Caribbean ports, including Brazil. The price of sugar sold to the United States is estimated from the price of raw sugar in New York by subtracting the U.S. tariff duty and the cost of transportation and insurance from the Caribbean area to New York. In recent years the cost of transportation and insurance has averaged about 0.4 cents per pound.

If a change in the U.S. sugar program would not result in any change in the quota premium, the average quota premium for a period of years could be used to estimate an important component of what the sugar program costs U.S. consumers. But if the United States adopted a free trade policy for sugar, the price of sugar in the world market would be increased. There are two reasons why the world market price—and thus the quota premium—would increase: First, U.S. imports would be increased due to an increase in consumption and a decline in domestic production, and, second, the world price of sugar does not represent a supply price that is reflected directly back to sugar producers.

Table 6 provides estimates of the quota premium for raw sugar for 1961 through 1973. The series starts with 1961 because that was the first year in which we received no sugar imports from Cuba. The table gives the two price series from which the quota premium is calculated—the return from sugar shipped to the United States and sugar sold on the world market. For the thirteen-year period the average return from sugar sold to the United States was 6.62 cents, the average world price 4.35 cents, and the average quota premium 2.27 cents. The range in the quota premium was very large—from a maximum of 4.56 cents in 1968 to a minimum of a *negative* 1.23 cents in 1963—a range of 5.79 cents per pound.

## The World Sugar Price

The world sugar price is not what one would call an ideal, competitive price that fully reflects underlying cost and demand conditions. A considerable fraction of sugar sold on the market is sugar that cannot be absorbed by preferential systems, such as the U.S. sugar program or the British Commonwealth scheme, or consumed in the producing countries, often in highly protected markets. Most sugar producing countries have considerable government control over the production and marketing of sugar. When a country has access to a preferential market, its government is likely to encourage a level of production that will always or almost always permit the sale of the country's full preferential quota and supply its domestic market as well. In most years there is some sugar in excess of the requirements for these two outlets, and much of the sugar that enters the world market is produced under such circumstances.

## Table 6

### UNITED STATES AND WORLD SUGAR PRICES, 1948-73 [a]

(U.S. cents per pound)

| Year | United States | World | Quota Premium |
|------|---------------|-------|---------------|
| 1948 | 4.64 | 4.23 | 0.41 |
| 49 | 4.94 | 4.16 | 0.78 |
| 1950 | 5.09 | 4.98 | 0.11 |
| 51 | 5.07 | 5.67 | −0.60 |
| 52 | 5.35 | 4.17 | 1.18 |
| 53 | 5.43 | 3.41 | 2.02 |
| 54 | 5.21 | 3.26 | 1.95 |
| 55 | 5.00 | 3.24 | 1.76 |
| 56 | 5.10 | 3.48 | 1.62 |
| 57 | 5.30 | 5.16 | 0.14 |
| 58 | 5.41 | 3.50 | 1.91 |
| 59 | 5.35 | 2.97 | 2.38 |
| 1960 | 5.35 | 3.14 | 2.21 |
| 61 | 5.36 | 2.91 | 2.45 |
| 62 | 5.56 | 2.98 | 2.58 |
| 63 | 7.27 | 8.50 | −1.23 |
| 64 | 5.98 | 5.87 | 0.11 |
| 65 | 5.80 | 2.12 | 3.68 |
| 66 | 6.03 | 1.86 | 4.17 |
| 67 | 6.32 | 1.99 | 4.33 |
| 68 | 6.54 | 1.98 | 4.56 |
| 69 | 6.75 | 3.37 | 3.38 |
| 1970 | 6.94 | 3.75 | 3.19 |
| 71 | 7.39 | 4.52 | 2.87 |
| 72 | 7.99 | 7.43 | 0.56 |
| 73 [b] | 8.65 | 9.31 | −0.66 |

[a] The prices represent the returns from sugar shipped from Cuba for 1948-1960 and for 1961 to date from greater-Caribbean ports (including Brazil). The column for the United States is calculated from the New York duty-paid price for raw sugar minus the duty and shipping costs to New York. The column called World represents the world market price. For further details, see source.

[b] January through September only.

**Source:** U.S. House of Representatives, Committee on Agriculture, *History and Operations of the U.S. Sugar Program,* 87th Congress, 2d session, 14 May 1962, p. 15, and Agricultural Stabilization and Conservation Service, U.S. Department of Agriculture, *Sugar Reports,* August 1973, p. 16, and later issues.

There are four countries that have or have had U.S. sugar quotas in recent years that sell significant amounts of sugar on the world market: Brazil, Australia, Taiwan, and South Africa. The first two sell less in the world market than they do to preferential markets, whereas Taiwan and South Africa have sold most of their sugar on the world market. But these two countries appear to be exceptions among the sugar producers.

In recent years approximately 12 percent of the world's sugar supply has moved on the world market.[2] The rest has been consumed within the country where produced or sold under one of the preferential arrangements. As noted above, the world market absorbs the fluctuations that occur because of the relatively stable demand for sugar in generally highly protected markets and worldwide variations in the supply of sugar. Since the world market has had an average volume of about eight million tons in recent years, a variation of only one million tons in the world demand and supply relationship for the remaining 65 to 70 million tons of raw sugar could increase or decrease the supply in the world market by more than 12 percent from one year to the next. Between 1968 and 1969, for example, the countries that export sugar to the U.S. decreased their exports to the world market by a million short tons or about 30 percent.[3] These countries supply approximately 40 percent of the sugar that goes onto the world market. The price in the world market in 1968 was 1.98 cents per pound; in 1969 it was 3.37 cents per pound.

Because so many countries control the price of sugar, the effects of variations in supply are not permitted to influence consumer prices, thus cushioning part of the effects of supply variations. When sugar supplies increase relative to the increase in demand, most countries do not permit their consumers to take advantage of the lower raw sugar price. Similarly, when sugar prices are high in the world market, consumer prices in the majority of the consuming markets change little, if at all, and thus, consumer prices do not serve to ration the available supplies.

One rather odd characteristic of the world market for sugar is that exporters have sold substantial quantities of sugar to the United States at prices below the world market price. This occurred in 1963 and again in 1973 (see Table 6). Such seemingly irrational behavior occurs because these exporters want to maintain long-run access to the U.S. market, as on the average, the returns from exports to the U.S. have been substantially greater than those on the world market. The exporters also know that the world market is "thin," that is, any significant diversion from the U.S. market to the world market would result in a major reduction in the world market price.

There are some countries that acquire all or nearly all of their imported sugar from the world market. Included in this group are Japan, with imports of 2.6 million short tons, Canada, with imports of about one million short tons, and several African and Asian countries that together import about 4 million tons.[4] Since Japan maintains a high and stable price of sugar in its domestic markets, it contributes directly to the instability of prices in the world market by preventing variations in the world price from being reflected in its domestic prices. On the other hand, Canada, displaying rare enlightenment, does permit its internal price to vary with the world market.

The world price for sugar is influenced by the pricing practices followed in most, if not all, sugar exporting countries. Generally the exporters pay producers the average price that is received for all sugar produced and sold. The producer price, net of refining and marketing costs, is thus an average of the price in the domestic market, exports to preferential markets, and exports to the world market. For example, in 1968 the average price in U.S. dollars received for raw sugar in Australia was $90.50 per metric ton. This was an average of a home consumption price of $157.85 and an average export price of $69.49. The average export price reflected the world price of $42 and the higher prices received for sales in the preferential markets of the United States and the United Kingdom.[5]

The world price for sugar cannot be said to be the supply price that brought forth the quantity of actual exports in recent years. Some part of the supply to the world market has been forthcoming because of the higher prices received in the preferential markets. Because of its importance as a sugar consumer and importer, any significant change in the U.S. sugar program would have an effect on the world price. There would be some effect on the world price even if the United States limited total sugar imports to the same volume as it would under the Sugar Act but taxed away the potential gain from foreign access to our market through a variable levy. The variable levy would reduce returns to sugar exporters, result in a reduction in the quantity supplied to the world market, and generate a higher world price.

In 1969 the countries that exported sugar to the United States exported a total of 10.55 million short tons. Of this amount 4.90 million tons went to the United States, 3.06 million tons to other preferential markets, and 2.60 million tons to the world market.[6] In that year the world price was $67.40 per ton; the return from sales to the United States was $135.00 per ton. If the U.S. taxed away the quota premium, the exporters would have lost $67.60 per ton or a total of $331 million. This would have reduced their average return on all sugar exported by $31.40 per ton. For the sugar exported to the U.S. plus the sugar sold on the world market the loss in average return would have been $44.16 per ton. Assuming that there were no change in the prices in the other preferential markets, the sugar exporters who supplied the U.S. imports would have required a world price of $111.56 per short ton to have provided the same total return for sugar as they received in 1969 from the U.S. preferential market and the world market. As indicated above, the world price in 1969 was $67.40 per short ton.

The above calculations are a rough indication of what the world price of sugar would have had to be in 1969 if the United States imported the same quantity of sugar and taxed away the value of the quota premium. The calculation assumes that none of the current suppliers of sugar limit production and that there are no low-cost suppliers of sugar who could have expanded their total exports for a marginal return of $111.56 per short ton. As will be noted later, Brazil and other important producers have been limiting sugar production and could expand production substantially. While the foregoing can hardly be considered conclusive, it does indicate that current or past values of the quota premium do not provide an accurate indication of the cost of the sugar program to U.S. consumers and taxpayers.

### Cycles in Sugar Production and Prices

There is a world sugar production cycle that varies in length from six to nine years. In the past two years we have witnessed a production trough and a price peak. The previous price peak was in 1963. For 1971 through 1973 the world consumption of sugar exceeded world production, and the difference has been made up by a draw down of stocks. It now appears that we are entering a new phase in the sugar cycle, with world production for 1973-74 now projected by the U.S. Department of Agriculture as greater than projected world consumption for the year. World production in recent years has averaged about 71 million metric tons.[7]

There are several factors affecting the sugar production cycle. The near stagnation in world production from 1971 through 1973 was a consequence of the very low world prices in 1966 through 1968. The price increases that occurred during 1969, 1970, and 1971 were hardly sufficient to encourage additional plantings of sugar cane. The plantings of sugar cane that were undertaken in response to the high sugar prices in 1972 are just now entering production. In most parts of the world the first harvest from newly planted sugar cane does not occur until fifteen to twenty-four months after planting.

Another factor contributing to the sugar cycle is that in most production areas sugar production from a single planting may occur over periods of from two to ten years duration. Consequently, new plantings can fall to a very low level while sugar cane output is maintained at a nearly constant level for a number of years by harvesting cane from fields planted a number of years before. However,

47

cane fields reach a peak yield within a few years and then, as the cane plants grow older, yields decline. Thus sugar cane output will gradually decline after one or two years if there are no new plantings.

The U.S. Department of Agriculture projects that world sugar production in 1973-74 may be as much as 82 million metric tons, up from 76 million metric tons in 1972-73.[8] It thus appears that the world sugar cycle is entering a new phase of increased output and declining prices. The rebuilding of stocks may limit price declines over the next year, but once stocks have been rebuilt, it is reasonable to expect a substantial decline in world sugar prices.

## Estimates of the World Price with Free Trade [9]

A review of the literature has revealed four estimates of the effect of free trade in sugar on the world price. R. W. Snape estimated that for 1959 the world price would have been increased from approximately three cents per pound to between 4 and 4.5 cents per pound.[10] It appears that Snape did not give sufficient consideration to the actual prices received for sugar by the exporting countries because he neglected the price benefits that exporting countries received from the preferential market.

A second estimate was made by Thomas H. Bates.[11] He estimated that in 1970 the average cost of sugar to the U.S. would have been 6.7 cents per pound with the sugar program and 4.8 cents in a free trade situation. These estimates were in terms of 1959 price levels. Bates's estimate of the average cost with the program was not far from the actual 1970 average price of raw sugar, which was 7.4 cents (excluding duty) in New York. Bates's estimates reflected the anticipated effects of population and income growth on the demand for sugar as well as the effects of free trade. Thus one cannot directly compare his projected 1970 world price of 4.8 cents per pound to the actual 1959 world price of 3.4 cents (delivered in New York, excluding duty).

The third set of estimates is for 1980, and was made by FAO.[12] Two projections of the world price were made, the first assuming a continuation of present policies and the second assuming free trade. In the first case, the world export price of sugar was estimated at five cents per pound; under free trade the estimate was 8.2 cents per pound.

The fourth estimate of the world price was made in the Flanigan report—a report prepared in the U.S. Department of Agriculture called *Agricultural Trade and the Proposed Round of Multilateral Negotiations*.[13] The estimate is a judgmental one made by knowledgeable persons. With free trade for sugar a world price of six cents per pound was projected. The estimate was based on the average world price of sugar for the most recent sugar cycle from 1963 through 1971 of 3.8 cents per pound plus something over two cents per pound to cover the full costs of production.

If there were free trade in sugar generally or if only the United States among the major industrial countries removed its import barriers, there would be a dramatic change in the world market for sugar. The amount of sugar moving in that market would at least double and could easily treble. Some of the increase would consist of a transfer from preferential markets while the rest would be a real increase in import demand. Thus it does not seem reasonable to use a single world price or a single quota premium as the basis for estimating the costs of the U.S. sugar program. In the next section I have used three different quota premiums, and I believe that the range of costs estimated gives a reasonable approximation of what the costs of the sugar program would have been in recent years if there had been time to adjust to an expansion in demand in the world market.

### Alternative Estimates of Consumer and Taxpayer Costs

The estimates in Table 7 are based on actual U.S. sugar prices and consumption levels in 1972. During that year the U.S. price of raw sugar was 9.09 cents per pound, duty paid. The price received by foreign producers in greater-Caribbean ports (including Brazil) for sugar sold to the United States was 7.99 cents per pound. The total consumption of raw sugar in 1972 was 11.4 million short tons. The tariff rate was 0.625 cents per pound and the excise tax 0.50 cents per pound, both in terms of raw sugar.

The critical element in the estimate of sugar program costs is the long-run supply of sugar as of the price and cost conditions of 1972. The projections of the world price of sugar summarized above assume worldwide free trade in sugar. The United States, of course, can only determine its own actions. The world price would be different if only the United States changed its sugar program. There are strong interests in the European Economic Community (EEC) that want to expand production within the EEC to displace part or all of the sugar imported by the United Kingdom.

In choosing the long-run supply price used to estimate the costs of the U.S. sugar program I quite deliberately selected a conservative base for the upper limit estimate, with two higher prices for the middle and lower estimates. Thus I believe that I have probably

## Table 7
## ALTERNATIVE ESTIMATES OF THE COST OF THE
## U.S. SUGAR PROGRAM, 1972

|  | Quota Premium (cents per pound) | | |
| --- | --- | --- | --- |
|  | 2.5 | 2.0 | 1.5 |
|  | million dollars | | |
| Consumer cost |  |  |  |
| Quota premium cost | 570.0 | 456.0 | 342.0 |
| Tariff cost | 142.5 | 142.5 | 142.5 |
| Excise tax cost | 114.0 | 114.0 | 114.0 |
| Total | 826.5 | 712.5 | 598.5 |
| Taxpayer cost |  |  |  |
| Receipts |  |  |  |
| Tariff | 64.1 | 64.1 | 64.1 |
| Excise tax | 114.0 | 114.0 | 114.0 |
| Total receipts | 178.1 | 178.1 | 178.1 |
| Less payments | 82.0 | 82.0 | 82.0 |
| Net cost | —96.1 | —96.1 | —96.1 |
| Net cost | 730.4 | 616.4 | 502.4 |

underestimated the long-run costs of the U.S. sugar program in Table 7. The higher estimate of cost is based on the projection of the 1970 world price of sugar made by Bates adjusted upward to reflect the change in U.S. wholesale prices between 1959 and 1972. Between 1959 and 1972 wholesale prices increased by 25.6 percent. Thus the projection of the landed cost of raw sugar for the United States of 4.78 cents in 1959 prices is increased to 6.0 cents per pound. This implies a world price at greater-Caribbean ports of approximately 5.5 cents per pound for raw sugar and a quota premium of 2.5 cents under 1972 conditions.[14] The middle estimate of the quota premium of 2.0 cents is based on a price of 6.0 cents per pound at the greater-Caribbean ports and is approximately the projection made in the Flanigan report. The lowest estimate of costs of the sugar program is based on a quota premium of 1.5 cents per pound.

The middle estimate of the quota premium implies a world price of raw sugar of $120 per ton. The higher quota premium implies a world price of $110 per ton and the lower quota premium $130 per ton. The landed price in the United States would be approximately $10 per ton greater than the world price, prior to the imposition of any duty. The "natural" protection of sugar that is provided by the cost of transportation from the major exporting area to the United States is not included as a factor in the cost of the sugar program.

As shown in Table 7, the estimates of annual consumer and taxpayer costs—the long-run annual cost of the U.S. sugar program for conditions as of 1972—range from $502 million to $730 million. It should be noted that during 1972 the quota premium was less than any included in Table 7, namely, 0.56 cents per pound. The world price of sugar in 1972 was 7.43 cents per pound, 66 percent above the 1971 price, which was in turn the highest world price of sugar since 1964.

# CHAPTER VII

# BENEFITS OF THE SUGAR PROGRAM

The sugar program is intended to protect and nourish the U.S. sugar industry and to provide the United States with a stable and secure supply of sugar. The objectives of the Sugar Act of 1948, as amended, are "to protect the welfare of consumers of sugars and of those engaged in the domestic sugar-producing industry," and "to promote the export trade of the United States."

In this chapter I shall consider how the monetary benefits of the sugar program are distributed among domestic and foreign sugar producers and between domestic producers and processors. In Chapter VIII I shall discuss the question of whether the United States could obtain a stable and secure supply of sugar with a different sugar program involving substantially lower costs to consumers and taxpayers.

**Distribution between Domestic and Foreign Sugar Producers**

As was noted earlier, one of the features of the sugar program is that foreign producers receive the U.S. domestic price of raw sugar, subject to a tariff of 0.625 cents per pound. If the long-run quota premium were two cents per pound, the total cost to consumers of the quota premium for both domestic and imported sugar would be $456 million if consumption of sugar (raw value) were 11.4 million tons. In 1972 the sugar supply consisted of 5 million tons of imported sugar and 6.4 million tons of domestic sugar. Thus, of the total value of the quota premium, $200 million went to foreign suppliers of raw sugar and $256 million to domestic suppliers.

However, domestic producers of cane and beets received income over and above the quota premium from two sources: the effect of the tariff on domestic sugar prices and the direct payments under the sugar program. The tariff increased returns to domestic producers by 0.625 cents per pound of raw sugar. In 1972 the payments averaged 0.64 cents per pound of raw sugar. In 1972 the gross returns from the tariff effect on prices of raw sugar produced in the United States was $80 million, and the direct payments totaled $82 million. The sum of the three sources of gross transfer to domestic producers—the quota premium, the tariff price effect, and the direct payments—was $418 million. The total gross transfer to domestic and foreign producers is $618 million, which differs slightly from the middle estimate in Table 7 due to small rounding errors.

### Total Farm Income from Domestic Production of Sugar

In 1972 sugar producers on the mainland and in Hawaii received $753.7 million from the sale of sugar cane and sugar beets. Producers in Puerto Rico had sales of $33.6 million.[1] Including producer payments under the sugar program, gross farm income from sugar production was $873 million. This total may be compared with the estimated cost of the program to consumers and taxpayers of $614 million (middle estimate) or the gross transfer under the sugar program to domestic producers of $418 million. Making these comparisons, we find that the cost of the sugar program to consumers and taxpayers is 75 percent of the gross income of domestic sugar producers, and the gross transfer to domestic producers is slightly more than half of their gross income from the sale of sugar cane and beets.

At first glance it might seem that the ratio of the gross transfer to domestic producers and the cash farm income from production of sugar cane and beets is rather high. As noted above, in this analysis the long-run quota premium is assumed to be two cents per pound. The additional protection to domestic producers totals 1.265 cents per pound from the tariff and direct payments, giving a total protection of 3.265 cents per pound of raw sugar recovered from domestically produced cane and beets. The price of raw sugar in 1972 was 9.07 cents per pound, duty paid. The nominal protection—the difference between the returns to domestic producers and the long-run equilibrium price in the world market—appears to be only a little more than a third of the domestic price of raw sugar.

This apparent anomaly is explained by the fact that farmers receive only a fraction of the value of raw sugar. In 1971, when the raw sugar price, duty paid, was 8.52 cents per pound, the price received by farmers for each pound of raw sugar ranged from 5.74

cents to 5.87 cents.[2] The approximate average for both cane and beet sugar was 5.80 cents per pound of raw sugar or 68 percent of the raw sugar price. If the same ratio applied to 1972 (at the time of writing prices paid to producers in 1972 had not been published), the return to farmers per pound of raw sugar would have been 6.17 cents. When the direct payment is added (0.64 cents per pound) the total return may be estimated at 6.81 cents per pound. As was noted above, the nominal protection was estimated to be 3.265 cents per pound or 48 percent of the price received by domestic producers.

This estimate of nominal protection at 48 percent differs slightly from the ratio of the gross transfer to domestic producers to their cash income because the calculations above have been made only for mainland producers. Because of the integration of the Hawaiian sugar industry, sugar cane price data are not published for Hawaii. In addition, producers in Puerto Rico received 6.31 cents per pound of raw sugar from both processor and government payments— somewhat less than the average for the mainland cane and beets.

In the estimates of the gross income transfer to sugar producers it has been assumed that all of the transfer went to farmers. This assumption is undoubtedly in error, though the magnitude of the error is unknown. Some of the gross transfer, or the nominal protection, almost certainly goes to sugar processors because of the virtual prohibition on the importation of refined sugar.

### Distribution of the Gross Transfer among Farmers

So far as I know, there has been no claim made that the sugar program was designed to improve the lot of the small farmer or to maintain the viability of the family farm. Yet I think that it is appropriate to ask how the gross income transfers under the program have been distributed among farms by size. Table 8 presents data on the per-farm acreage of sugar cane or beets and the per-farm gross income from sugar sales and Sugar Act payments in 1972.

The range in average per-farm income sugar sales is enormous: from $9,495 in Puerto Rico to $576,385 in Florida. There are three states—Utah, Michigan, and Ohio—in which the per-farm sales were less than $14,000. Thus the state with the highest per-farm sales had more than forty times the sales of the states with the lowest per-farm sales.

Since the payments under the sugar program are graduated, with the highest rate of payment going to farms with the lowest level of output, the range in the per-farm level of payments is somewhat smaller than for cash income. However, in Florida the payment

## Table 8

NUMBER OF FARMS AND PER-FARM AVERAGES OF ACREAGE
HARVESTED, SUGAR SOLD, GOVERNMENT PAYMENTS
AND INCOME FROM SUGAR, 1972 [a]

(dollars)

| State | Number of Farms | Acreage Harvested Per Farm | Income from Sugar Per Farm | | |
|---|---|---|---|---|---|
| | | | Sugar sold | Payments | Total |
| Florida | 140 | 1,739 | 576,385 | 43,471 | 619,856 |
| Hawaii | 410 | 264 | 285,853 | 26,758 | 312,611 |
| Louisiana | 1,438 | 217 | 69,092 | 5,997 | 75,089 |
| Puerto Rico | 3,535 | 43 | 9,495 | 1,143 | 10,638 |
| Arizona | 54 | 178 | 67,611 | 6,759 | 74,370 |
| California | 1,423 | 235 | 96,391 | 10,731 | 107,122 |
| Idaho | 2,228 | 74 | 25,256 | 3,372 | 28,628 |
| Oregon | 266 | 76 | 29,969 | 3,590 | 33,559 |
| Washington | 866 | 90 | 42,324 | 4,561 | 46,885 |
| Colorado | 1,785 | 78 | 23,970 | 2,950 | 26,920 |
| Iowa | 19 | 94 | — | 2,632 | — |
| Kansas | 220 | 177 | 55,345 | 6,150 | 61,495 |
| Minnesota | 990 | 113 | 30,077 | 4,024 | 34,101 |
| Montana | 649 | 72 | 23,305 | 3,179 | 26,484 |
| Nebraska | 1,135 | 68 | 22,350 | 2,977 | 25,327 |
| New Mexico | 9 | 67 | — | 2,778 | — |
| North Dakota | 761 | 97 | 26,833 | 3,628 | 30,461 |
| Texas | 226 | 89 | 39,823 | 3,903 | 43,726 |
| Utah | 670 | 37 | 12,294 | 1,640 | 13,934 |
| Wyoming | 658 | 94 | 30,340 | 4,122 | 34,462 |
| Michigan | 2,050 | 40 | 10,184 | 1,515 | 11,699 |
| Ohio | 936 | 43 | 13,590 | 1,577 | 15,167 |

[a] Data on farm numbers and acreage harvested per farm for beet areas are for 1971. Income from sugar per farm calculated from 1972 income and 1971 number of farms.

**Source:** Agricultural Stabilization and Conservation Service, U.S. Department of Agriculture, *Sugar Reports,* January 1973, February 1973 and April 1973.

per farm was almost thirty times the payment in Ohio and was nearly forty times the average for Puerto Rico.

The four states with $75,000 or more of per-farm total cash income from sugar generated nearly 60 percent of the total domestically produced sugar in 1972. These four states together had 3,411 farms that produced sugar in 1971 out of a total 21,000 such farms in the United States. In fact, the concentration of production is even greater than indicated: 224 farms in Hawaii, Louisiana, Florida, and Puerto Rico produce at least a third of all U.S. sugar.[3] Large farms clearly dominate sugar production, and it is large farms that derive most of the benefits from the sugar program.

## Gross Benefits, Employment and Wages

Table 9 presents data on the peak number of production workers, hourly earnings, total wages and salaries, and the annual number of hours worked in sugar production and processing in the United States. For 1971 the total wages and salaries were $494 million, which may be compared with the gross transfer to domestic sugar producers of $418 million. The estimate of wages and salaries includes the work performed by farm operators and their families calculated at the average wage rate paid to hired farm workers.

### Table 9

EMPLOYMENT, HOURS WORKED, HOURLY EARNINGS AND
WAGES AND SALARIES, U.S. SUGAR INDUSTRY,
1962, 1966, 1970 AND 1971

| Group | Year | Production Workers [a] (thousands) | Total Annual Hours Worked [b] (millions) | Average Hourly Earnings (dollars) | Total Wages and Salaries (million dollars) |
|---|---|---|---|---|---|
| Farms | 1962 | 230.8 | 195.2 | 0.92 | 179.6 |
| | 1966 | 195.2 | 194.7 | 1.17 | 227.8 |
| | 1970 | 129.1 | 122.8 | 1.84 | 226.0 |
| | 1971 | 120.1 | 111.9 | 2.02 | 226.1 |
| Raw cane mills | 1962 | 21.7 | 30.1 | 1.67 | 50.2 |
| | 1966 | 17.9 | 29.4 | 2.15 | 63.3 |
| | 1970 | 17.1 | 24.6 | 2.75 | 67.6 |
| | 1971 | 16.0 | 23.9 | 2.94 | 70.2 |
| Cane sugar refineries | 1962 | 14.7 | 29.0 | 3.07 | 89.0 |
| | 1966 | 9.6 | 24.2 | 3.64 | 88.1 |
| | 1970 | 9.3 | 23.8 | 4.28 | 101.7 |
| | 1971 | 13.1 | 25.1 | 4.33 | 108.6 |
| Beet sugar processors | 1962 | 25.4 | 24.5 | 2.26 | 55.3 |
| | 1966 | 23.9 | 25.0 | 2.71 | 67.7 |
| | 1970 | 23.8 | 27.3 | 3.15 | 86.4 |
| | 1971 | 26.6 | 25.9 | 3.44 | 89.1 |
| Total | 1962 | 292.6 | 278.8 | 1.34 | 374.1 |
| | 1966 | 246.6 | 273.3 | 1.64 | 446.9 |
| | 1970 | 179.3 | 198.5 | 2.44 | 481.7 |
| | 1971 | 175.8 | 186.8 | 2.64 | 494.0 |

[a] The number of production workers is the peak number of workers—not an annual average. Figures for farms include hired workers, farm operators and unpaid family workers. Processing sector includes production workers only.

[b] Estimated by dividing total of wages and salaries by hourly earnings; total hours worked includes hired farm workers, operators and unpaid family workers.

**Source:** Agricultural Stabilization and Conservation Service, U.S. Department of Agriculture, *Sugar Reports,* August 1972 and August 1973.

The data in the first two columns of Table 9 indicate that employment is highly seasonal on farms and in beet sugar processing plants, for they show that average annual employment is only approximately 1,000 hours per production worker. In raw cane mills employment averages about 1,500 hours per worker per year, while employment in cane sugar refineries appears to be rather steady throughout the year.

With one exception—farm workers in Hawaii—it does not appear that workers have gained significantly from the sugar program. The domestic raw cane mills are located in Florida and Louisiana. In 1971 the average hourly earnings for manufacturing workers was $3.07 in Florida and $3.46 in Louisiana, somewhat more than the hourly earnings in the rather seasonal raw cane mills. Beet sugar processors are located in several states, including Michigan, Colorado, Idaho, and California. In these states average manufacturing production worker hourly earnings in 1971 were $4.50, $3.74, $3.54, and $4.02 respectively. In each of the cited states the average hourly earnings for manufacturing were above the national average for sugar beet processors. Average hourly earnings in sugar cane refining appear to be higher than manufacturing production worker earnings in the states where cane sugar refineries are located.

The very significant decline in the number of farm workers engaged in sugar production between 1962 and 1971 indicates that gains to farm workers, if any, must have been very small. In all domestic areas, except Florida, there has also been a significant decline in the number of farm operators engaged in the production of sugar. This implies that, if there have been substantial economic benefits from producing sugar, they have been capitalized into the value of land and not in the return to labor. But much of the decline in farm employment has apparently been in hired farm workers.

### The Net Benefits

I have so far discussed the gross transfers, or benefits, from the sugar program. I believe that the net benefits—the net increase in income going to farm-owned resources—are only a small fraction of the gross benefits. Most of the gross transfers are required because the U.S. is a high-cost producer of sugar. Many resources are used in sugar production that would readily find employment elsewhere if less sugar were produced in the United States. Much of the gross transfer is required to induce these resources to be devoted to sugar production rather than their next best alternative.

58

**Figure 1**
NET INCOME TRANSFERS TO FARMERS

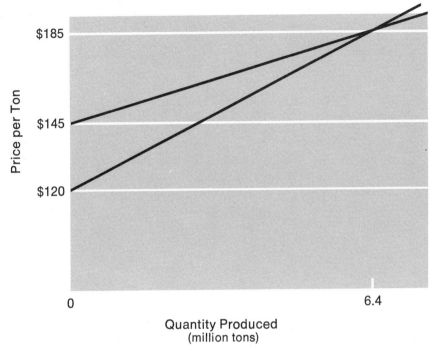

Quantity Produced
(million tons)

If we had a good estimate of the supply function or functions for domestic sugar production, it would be relatively easy to estimate the net income benefits from sugar production. Unfortunately, we do not have such estimates even for changes in prices of modest magnitudes—such as 10 percent—let alone over the range that might be involved if we had free trade in sugar. In 1972 U.S. producers received approximately $185 per ton of raw sugar derived from cane or beets produced. Under free trade the long-run expected price might be $120 per ton or more than a third less than the 1972 return.

Figure 1 provides two illustrations of what the net income benefits might be, given certain assumptions. In one case it is assumed that domestic sugar production would be eliminated at a farm price of $120 per ton of raw sugar, and in the other case it is assumed that such production would cease at a farm price of $145 per ton. In both instances the supply function is assumed to be linear. The net income benefit is the area above the supply function and below the price line of $185 per ton.

For the lower supply function, with domestic production being eliminated at a price of $120 per ton, the net income benefit in the illustration is $213 million if the domestic output level were 6.4 million tons at a farm price of $185 per ton of raw sugar. Thus the net income benefit is half of the gross income transfer to domestic producers. For the upper supply function the net income benefit is $128 million or only 30 percent of the gross income transfer.

The areas under the supply functions down to the price line of $120 per ton represent the excess resource costs of producing sugar in the United States instead of importing an equivalent amount of sugar and exporting products or services to pay for it. In these two illustrations the "waste" of resources from the sugar program would range from $215 million to $390 million.

As I shall indicate later in this chapter, I believe the net income benefit to the agricultural sector does not exceed $128 million. This does not mean that I believe sugar production would disappear in the United States with the advent of a $120 per ton farm price for raw sugar. However, as may be inferred from what is set forth below, it does mean that I believe domestic output would probably be very small at such a price and not very substantial until the price was at or above $160 per ton.

How much of the $418 million or 3.265 cents per pound of raw sugar remains as net income benefits to the producers of sugar? No exact answer to that question is possible, but some approximations can be given. I shall now present some general information as background before attempting to provide the rough range of the possible net benefits. Sugar beets and sugar cane will be considered separately because of important differences between the two crops.

**Sugar Beets.** I attempted a number of regression analyses to determine the effect of sugar beet growing on the price of farmland. If the production of sugar beets were significantly more profitable than the production of alternative crops, much of the extra profitability would be capitalized into the value of farmland. In effect, the rights to grow sugar beets are attached to a particular farm, and when these farms are sold (or their value estimated) the expected extra profits from producing sugar beets should influence the land price.[4]

The regression analyses were based on census data for 1959, 1964, and 1969. All counties in which any significant amount of sugar beets was produced were included. The data used included total farm sales, value of sugar produced, percentage of cropland in sugar beets, percentage of cropland irrigated, and percentage of total land in crops. In none of the regressions was there a significant relationship between the value of sugar beets produced or the percentage of cropland in sugar beets and the per-acre value of farmland. Nor was any significant relationship found between the changes in the value of farmland between 1959 and 1964 and changes in the value of sugar beets produced or changes in the percentage of cropland devoted to sugar beets. In some cases the coefficients of the value of sugar beets sold or the percentage of cropland in sugar beets were negative, but none were significantly different from zero.

I must admit that these results surprised me. I had expected to find some positive effect. I would not have been surprised if an acre of sugar beets added from $500 to $1,000 to the value of a farm. There has been considerable political pressure to establish new sugar beet producing areas, and it seemed reasonable to assume that farmers expected to gain from these efforts.

There are other data that are quite consistent with the regression results. For example, the 1962 amendments to the Sugar Act of 1948 provided for the establishment of new sugar beet areas. Of the six localities to be served by new facilities, two can be classed as complete failures. The plants were constructed but it was not possible to obtain enough sugar beets to operate the plants. These were plants in New York and Maine. A third plant was located in Phoenix, Arizona, and while the sugar beet acreage did initially develop to meet the area set for the plant, in recent years the acreage has been only about half that established for the plant. These comments are not conclusive evidence with respect to the profitability of sugar beets since the plant location choices could have been very poor ones. Three other new plants (California, North Dakota, and Texas) have been successful.[5]

The Sugar Act authorizes the secretary of agriculture to assign proportionate shares to individual farms if the output of sugar beets is expected to exceed the basic quota assigned to the domestic area. Such proportionate quotas have not been in effect since 1966.[6] While it is possible that some sugar beet processing plants have placed some restraint on the acreage planted by the producers that sell to them, this seems to be an unlikely possibility for most sugar refiners since for the past three years the adjusted final quotas for sugar beets have been less than the basic quotas provided for in the Sugar Act.

The patterns of change in acreage planted to and prices for sugar beets over the past several years do not indicate that the production of sugar beets has been especially profitable for farmers, particularly since 1969. The harvested acreage of sugar beets increased from 1,077,000 in 1961 to 1,395,000 in 1964. Harvested sugar beet acreage then declined to 1,161,000 in 1966, but rose to 1,563,000 in 1969.

It has since declined to 1,239,700 in 1973. Since there has been no explicit control of sugar beet acreage since 1966, the changes are consistent with what one would expect from a crop whose profitability varied from year to year and whose profitability was, at least for many producers, approximately the same as for the alternative uses of the resources. Between 1966 and 1969 the return per pound of raw sugar increased by 14 percent, while the prices farmers received for food grains declined by 15 percent and those for feed grains and hay declined by 7 percent.[7] Thus the positive acreage response from 1966 to 1969, given the significant increase in relative prices, was hardly surprising. From 1969 through 1971 the return per pound of sugar increased by about 10 percent. The prices received for food grains and feed grains (unweighted average) increased by approximately 14 percent. Yet the harvested acreage of sugar beets declined by almost 15 percent during the same period. Other factors than the small change in relative prices were obviously important: the sugar beet yield was low in 1969, though it did recover in 1970, and changes in the wheat and feed grain programs greatly reduced the acreage diverted in 1971 compared to 1970 and 1969. But, if sugar beets had been a crop with a distinct and substantial margin of profitability over alternative uses of land, labor, and other resources, such small changes in incentives should not have induced a 15 percent reduction in acreage between 1969 and 1971.

The sugar beet acreage harvested in 1972 was almost the same as in 1971, but the 1973 acreage was 6 percent below 1972. There were very substantial increases in grain prices in the spring of 1973, but it is not possible to say how far the planting plans for sugar beets had gone by the time it was evident that grain prices for the 1973 crops would be very high by past standards.

In the foregoing discussion I have emphasized the acreage of sugar beets rather than the production of sugar beets. (The production of sugar from beets was relatively stable from 1968 through 1972, though both acreage and yield declined in 1973.) This emphasis on the land devoted to sugar beets has been purposeful, for the excess returns, if any, from sugar production would accrue primarily to land. There is no reason why farmers would accept different returns from fertilizer or any other factor of production applied to sugar beets and some alternative crop. The continuing increase in sugar beet yield is not inconsistent with normal earnings from the production of sugar beets—overall crop yields have increased nationally over the same period of time. Once the decision is made to grow a given acreage of sugar beets, the farmer seeks to maximize the return from the area just as he does for a given acreage of wheat, corn, or alfalfa. The primary profitability decision for the farmer is the decision on the acreage of sugar beets relative to alternative uses of land. And the sum of such decisions indicates that, in general, sugar beets have not been more profitable than the alternative uses of land over the past few years.

The changes in acreage harvested and relative product prices are consistent with the finding in a study made by the U.S. Department of Agriculture in 1961 that the elasticity of acreage harvested of sugar beets ranged from 2.7 to 3.2.[8] Again, an acreage supply elasticity in this range is not one that would be associated with a very high return to resources with a comparative advantage in the production of a particular crop.

Table 10 gives data on harvested sugar beet acreages by states for six recent years. Only one state—Washington—increased acreage harvested between 1969 and 1973. Even North Dakota and Minnesota, which were each given sugar beet allocations of 30,000 acres effective in 1974, had substantial reductions in acreage between 1969 and 1973.[9]

F. J. Hills and S. S. Johnson of the University of California, Davis, have developed approximations of the total cost of producing sugar beets in three California counties for 1971. (As indicated in Table 10, California has the largest sugar beet acreage of any state.) In what was a relatively low-cost area, the annual costs, including land rent at a 20 percent share of the crop, per acre were $273.45. If the yield were twenty tons per acre, the average cost per ton was $13.67. Including Sugar Act payments, the return per ton of sugar beets was $17.14, implying a net "profit" of $3.47 per ton or $69.40 per acre. However, Hills and Johnson found that in two other important sugar beet counties, average costs were approximately $16.50 per ton, and the profit in these counties was clearly quite small.[10]

Robert A. Young of Michigan State University estimated that for 1966 the return to management and risk-bearing for sugar beets was approximately $42 per acre over the next best alternative in Michigan, and $37 per acre over the next best alternative in Ohio. These results seem consistent with the growth in sugar beet acreage from 1964 to 1969 and the relatively small percentage decline in acreage between 1969 and 1973 in these states. But it appears that similar calculations made for 1973 would indicate a smaller margin favorable to sugar beets, or else the acreage would not have declined after 1969.[11]

# Table 10

## ACREAGE OF SUGAR BEETS AND SUGAR CANE HARVESTED, UNITED STATES, SELECTED YEARS

(thousands of acres)

|  | 1963 | 1964 | 1968 | 1969 | 1971 | 1973 |
|---|---|---|---|---|---|---|
| **Beet sugar** | | | | | | |
| Arizona | — | — | 16.9 | 30.8 | 9.6 | 13.0 |
| California | 305.8 | 351.4 | 254.2 | 305.0 | 333.8 | 278.0 |
| Idaho | 145.6 | 174.7 | 182.3 | 185.6 | 163.8 | 146.0 |
| Nevada | 1.2 | 2.8 | — | — | — | — |
| Oregon | 19.3 | 20.3 | 22.0 | 23.8 | 20.1 | 19.0 |
| Washington | 63.9 | 59.4 | 54.9 | 64.0 | 78.2 | 93.0 |
| Colorado | 170.8 | 177.4 | 168.2 | 180.7 | 138.9 | 116.0 |
| Iowa | 4.7 | 4.0 | — | — | 1.6 | — |
| Kansas | 19.0 | 23.5 | 39.1 | 40.4 | 39.0 | 33.0 |
| Minnesota | 118.1 | 119.5 | 161.4 | 164.3 | 111.6 | 130.0 |
| Montana | 65.7 | 69.6 | 65.7 | 67.5 | 46.7 | 47.0 |
| Nebraska | 83.1 | 85.8 | 71.8 | 87.3 | 77.7 | 75.0 |
| New Mexico | — | 2.5 | — | — | 0.6 | — |
| North Dakota | 50.5 | 51.1 | 87.2 | 95.1 | 73.7 | 78.0 |
| South Dakota | 12.5 | 11.0 | — | — | — | — |
| Texas | 2.3 | 25.9 | 37.9 | 37.5 | 20.2 | 21.0 |
| Utah | 24.9 | 32.8 | 29.3 | 31.8 | 24.8 | 18.0 |
| Wyoming | 57.5 | 63.9 | 62.1 | 67.4 | 61.7 | 55.0 |
| Illinois | 1.0 | 1.2 | — | — | — | — |
| Maine | — | 0.1 | — | — | — | — |
| Michigan | 78.1 | 84.8 | 90.0 | 92.6 | 82.6 | 87.0 |
| New York | 0.3 | 0.1 | — | — | — | — |
| Ohio | 29.1 | 30.1 | 36.0 | 38.1 | 41.2 | 30.0 |
| **Beet total** | 1,253.4 | 1,391.9 | 1,379.0 | 1,511.6 | 1,325.8 | 1,239.0 |
| **Cane sugar** | | | | | | |
| Florida | 142.5 | 219.8 | 181.4 | 153.6 | 189.9 | 273.0 |
| Louisiana | 295.5 | 325.3 | 282.4 | 236.0 | 301.4 | 342.0 |
| Texas | — | — | — | — | — | 25.7 |
| Hawaii | 107.4 | 110.8 | 113.5 | 113.2 | 115.8 | 117.0 |
| **Cane total** | 545.4 | 655.9 | 577.3 | 502.8 | 607.1 | 757.7 |

**Source:** U.S. Department of Agriculture, *Agricultural Statistics* (Washington, D. C.: Government Printing Office), 1965, 1966, 1970, 1972, and U.S. Department of Agriculture, *Crop Production,* 9 November 1973.

The conclusion that there are not large net income benefits from the production of sugar beets in the United States is clearly implied by a recent article by A. Viton, service chief, Sugar, Beverages, and Horticultural Crops Service of the FAO and a frequent contributor to

*Sugar y Azucar*, a trade journal for the sugar industry. He concludes an article entitled "The Escalating Price of Sugar" as follows:

> Your author can see good economic and technical reasons to expect the real price of sugar to rise faster in the coming years in developed beet countries than in tropical cane countries. Unless there are major changes on the agricultural side, the potentialities for affecting reductions in production costs seem to be small and limited. In some parts of the U.S., beet cultivation is already declining in the face of soybeans, grain and other crops, the cultivation of which involves less trouble and the prices of which have risen sharply.[12]

The regression results—the failure to find a significant relationship between the acreage of sugar beets and land values—may be explained by the relative unimportance of sugar beets in the counties in which they are grown. Out of the approximately 150 counties in which sugar beets were grown in 1969, there were only fourteen counties in which more than 10 percent of all harvested cropland was devoted to sugar beets. Furthermore, only a relatively small percentage of the farmers in the counties that grow sugar beets are involved in sugar beet production. There are eleven counties that produced 400,000 tons or more of sugar beets in 1969. These counties had 20,592 commercial farms, of which 3,248—or 15.8 percent—grew sugar beets.[13]

**Sugar Cane.** There are fairly significant differences in the profitability of production among the four domestic sugar cane areas—Louisiana, Florida, Hawaii, and Puerto Rico. Thus each area must be considered separately.

*Puerto Rico.* Puerto Rico has not supplied the amount of sugar permitted by its quota since 1956. In 1961 the raw sugar produced was 1,109,000 tons; in 1971-72 production was only 298,000 tons. In 1961 there were 14,230 farms growing sugar; in 1971-72 only 3,535. This is a far larger decline in the number of sugar producing farms than in any of the other domestic producing areas. The number of farm workers engaged in sugar production has declined by almost 70 percent in the last decade.[14]

It is not altogether clear, at least to me, why sugar production has declined in Puerto Rico. Disease problems are apparently involved, and sugar yields, even with the much reduced area, have declined by about a third in the past decade, while in the other domestic areas yields have risen. Another and related factor may be the much greater increase in labor costs per ton of raw sugar in Puerto Rico as compared to the other domestic areas. The estimated cost of labor per ton of raw sugar in Puerto Rico in 1971 was $77 per ton compared to $34 to $48 in the other three areas. In 1960 the labor costs per ton were $49 in Puerto Rico and $24 to $40 in the other areas. The increase in Puerto Rico was 57 percent and ranged from 29 to 41 percent in the three states.[15] Whatever the reasons for the declining sugar production in Puerto Rico, it is fairly obvious that in the present circumstances there are no substantial extra income benefits being derived from its production.

*Hawaii.* Whatever net economic benefits there may be from the sugar program to Hawaiian sugar producers, most go to very few. In 1964 there were 705 farms that harvested sugar in Hawaii, and the total harvested area was 110,000 acres. However, in the same year, only twenty-five farms were responsible for 93 percent of the sugar cane area harvested, and the average area harvested on these farms was 4,112 acres, whereas the average for all farms was 157 acres.[16]

By some odd coincidence, even though sugar cane is the source of more than half of all cash from receipts in Hawaii, there is not a single statistic for sugar for that state in the 1969 *Census of Agriculture*. While the 1969 *Census of Agriculture* included much less data on sugar than did the 1959 and 1964 censuses, some data on sugar were given for all other states. In 1964 the same data were provided for Hawaii as for other states. Perhaps the fact that the county data for 1964 revealed that three farms in Maui produced an average of 727,000 tons of sugar cane worth approximately $650,000 may have had something to do with the failure to provide such data for 1969.[17] In two other counties—Honolulu and Kauai—average sales per farm were approximately 200,000 tons.

It may also be noted that data on the distribution of the size of farms producing sugar cane were at one time provided in *Sugar Reports* for each of the four domestic producing areas. Data are still being provided for Louisiana, Florida, and Puerto Rico, but the last such data on Hawaii were for 1966. It is obvious that, if such data can be obtained for the other areas, it is available for Hawaii—or could be available if there were any interests in the Sugar Division of the Agricultural Stabilization and Conservation Service of the U.S. Department of Agriculture.

The sugar cane acreage harvested in Hawaii has been relatively constant for the past decade, within a range of 107,000 to 116,000 acres. Acreage has not been limited directly under the sugar program.[18] However, I do not think anything can be inferred about the profitability of sugar cane production from the stability of acreage in the absence of the establishment of the proportionate farm shares. Because of the small number of farms producing the bulk of the sugar it is possible that private means are used to adjust sugar output to almost exactly fit the amount of sugar that can be shipped to the mainland. And the amount shipped or released from stocks has exactly filled the adjusted final quota for Hawaii every year since 1963. It may well be—though this is pure speculation—that certain private interests do not want the secretary of agriculture meddling in what they consider to be their problem: division of the rights to produce sugar.

I stated above that the net economic benefits from the sugar program to Hawaiian sugar producers go to relatively few. I was referring solely to the benefits that go to land, capital, management, and the labor of farm operators and their families. It should be noted that field worker wages in Hawaii are at least double those paid on the mainland. In 1971 hourly earnings were $3.44 plus fringe benefits of $1.28. Hourly earnings in the beet area were $2.04, in the Louisiana cane area $1.71, and in the Florida cane area $2.25. At least in part as a response to the higher wage rates, sugar yields per acre and per man-hour are much higher in Hawaii than in the mainland cane areas.[19] Thus it is quite possible that some of the economic rent from sugar production in Hawaii has been captured by approximately 5,000 farm workers.

Because of the lack of data it is not possible to estimate the net returns to land and other capital resources devoted to sugar production in Hawaii. The growth in Hawaiian sugar production since 1966 has been nil. At the U.S. House of Representatives committee hearings in 1971 the representative of the domestic industry recommended that the basic quota for Hawaii remain unchanged at the level specified in 1965. The recommendation of the domestic industry was that all of the 65 percent of consumption growth in excess of 11,200,000 tons should go to the mainland cane and beet areas and none to Hawaii.[20] All of the recommendations of the domestic industry on the allocations of quotas to domestic areas were met in the legislation enacted. There was a provision in the 1971 amendments that, if Hawaiian sugar production exceeded its fixed quota of 1,110,000 tons in any year, the excess could be shipped to the mainland "except that in no event shall the quota for Hawaii . . . as so increased, exceed the quota which would have been established for such area at the same level needed to meet the requirements of consumers under the provisions of this subsection in effect immediately prior to the date of enactment of the Sugar Act Amendments of 1962." [21] This provision permits a modest output increase for Hawaii.

I interpret the posture taken by the domestic industry in its legislative recommendations, which included a substantial increase in the quotas for the mainland cane areas (300,000 tons of sugar plus a definite share in the growth of consumption), as indicating that there was no great pressure from Hawaiian producers for increased production. If the return to sugar production were significantly in excess of the returns from alternative uses, it would have been reasonable for the Hawaiian producers to have asked to share in the increase in quotas assigned to the mainland cane areas. This presumption, plus the failure of Hawaiian output to increase in recent years, lends credence to the view that sugar production does not provide economic returns much, if at all, in excess of other available alternatives.

The columns of *Sugar y Azucar* during 1972 and 1973 presented several information items that are fully consistent with the conclusion that sugar production, including refining, is not earning unusual profits in Hawaii. First, in March 1972 it was reported that Robert R. Grunsky, as a spokesman for the sugar plantations, said "net profits dropped from $13 million in 1968 to an estimated $10 million in 1971. At the same time costs continued to climb. Grunsky said four sugar companies (not including Kilauea and Kahuku which closed at year-end) lost money last year. A fifth had profits of less than $10,000." [22] The total number of companies involved was not more than twenty-three. The $10 million profit in 1971—which I assume was after taxes—amounted to $8.15 per ton of raw sugar produced. This would have to cover the returns from growing and at least the production of raw sugar. Since there is a substantial non-land capital investment, the extra returns left over for land had to be very small.

Second, in addition to the two 1971 plantation closings referred to above, a third plantation, operated by the Kahala Sugar Company, a subsidiary of Castle and Cooke, was reported prepared to close at the end of the 1973 season. [23] Because of local pressure over the loss of employment, the closing of Kahala plantation has been delayed until the end of the 1974 season. [24]

Third, a report on the net profits of three subsidiaries of Theo H. Davies & Co. for 1971 showed net profits of $1,996,000 on the processing of 133,400 tons of raw sugar from cane. This is an average net profit of $15 per ton. [25]

And finally, in July 1973 C. E. S. Burns, senior vice president of Amfac, Inc., the largest sugar producer in Hawaii, made the following statement: "No sugar plantation, no matter how big or efficient, can afford to farm lands yielding less than eight tons of sugar per acre, and at 8.5 tons, the operation is marginal. Amfac has lots of acres, producing less than eight tons." [26] The average yield in Hawaii has been relatively stable for the past decade at 10.2 to 11.1 tons.

It appears that the sugar program is not resulting in gross income from sugar that is much in excess of the costs. Thus the net benefits are small, certainly a small fraction of the $65 per ton that the program costs the U.S. consumer and taxpayer.

*Louisiana and Florida.* After a short period of adjustment to the significant quota increase in the early 1960s, the mainland cane area met its quota annually. Deliveries increased from approximately 600,000 tons annually in 1959 and 1960 to more than a million tons in 1973.[27] The increase in production has been much larger in Florida than in Louisiana. In fact, since 1963 production in Louisiana has fluctuated from year to year with no apparent trend. Output in Florida has had a distinct upward trend, due more to increasing yields than additional acreage. Proportionate shares have been in effect for the mainland cane area, and consequently, the output behavior in Louisiana cannot be used for any inference concerning the relative profitability of sugar cane production. It is quite clear that sugar production has been considered profitable in Florida.

For a number of reasons, it was not possible to undertake a regression analysis of land values in Florida and Louisiana to estimate the effects of the sugar program on net returns. There are only three sugar cane producing counties in Florida. In the county that contained 69 percent of the state's harvested sugar cane area in 1969 (Palm Beach), land values seem to be significantly affected by the county's location. In 1969 Louisiana had only thirteen parishes with more than 5 percent of the total farm area in harvested cane.[28]

The available data do not permit a direct estimate of any extra returns from the production of sugar for Louisiana and Florida. It is undoubtedly quite substantial since the alternative uses of land now devoted to sugar cane are, in most cases, quite limited. The Parish of St. Mary in Louisiana may be used as an illustration. In 1959 its average cane yield was above the state average and in 1964 a little below. No data are available for 1969. In 1969 the value per acre of all land and buildings in the parish was $398.[29] Approximately 30 percent of the farm area was harvested sugar cane cropland, with an additional 12 percent in sugar cane too young to harvest.[30] The cash return from all sources was $76 per acre, of which $70 was estimated to come from sugar cane. If all of the net rent came from sugar cane, and if it is assumed that a discount rate of 6 percent was used, then the per-acre rent to all farmland in that parish was about $24 and about $80 per acre of sugar cane harvested. It is highly probable that in this parish, if sugar cane production were not profitable, the value of land and the level of employment would decline by a major fraction.

Much of the sugar cane in Louisiana is grown on rented land and on a share basis.[31] The land ownership appears to be rather widely distributed: in 1971 there were 4,919 payees under the sugar program and only 1,513 producing farms.[32] This implies that there were perhaps as many as 3,400 landlords who received payments from the program.[33] The limited data that are available indicate that most of the net income benefits from the sugar program go to land owners, which is what one would expect economic analysis to show.

The increased output of sugar cane in Florida has been largely due to a fairly small number of relatively large farms. In 1971-72 there were forty-nine farms with more than 500 acres of sugar cane planted (the area harvested plus that abandoned). These farms were responsible for approximately 92 percent of the total Florida sugar cane acreage, and averaged almost 3,880 acres per farm.[34]

Cane yields in Florida are approximately 50 percent greater than in Louisiana, in part because natural conditions are more favorable. It seems unlikely that the net return to land could exceed 30 percent of the gross receipts of $403 per acre harvested ($135). If this were the net income benefit it would require that the land had no alternative use other than the production of sugar cane. Given the location of the land and the diversified character of the agriculture in two of the three counties that produce sugar cane in Florida, a more reasonable upper limit of the net income benefits is $100 per acre of sugar cane harvested.

## Summary of Estimated Income Benefits

From the rather impressionistic analysis presented above I have attempted to develop upper limit estimates of the net income benefits from the production of sugar. The estimates should not be taken too seriously, and are subject to correction as additional information becomes available.

The net income benefits to farmers in Puerto Rico are clearly very small, and even if the sugar program were continued in its present form, sugar production probably will continue to decline. I have assumed that the net income benefits for Puerto Rico are nil. The net income benefits for the sugar beet area appear to be quite small: for this exercise I estimate the upper limit as $10 per ton of raw sugar ($26 per acre of sugar beets harvested). Obviously, the extra marginal income varies among the sugar beet producing areas. The upper limit estimates for Hawaii are $10 per ton for the producers and the same amount per ton for the workers, for a total of $200 per acre harvested. The estimate for Louisiana is $80 per acre and for Florida $100 per acre. All the estimates are on an annual basis and are based on 1971 acreages.

The upper limit estimates (in millions of dollars) may be summarized as follows:

| | |
|---|---|
| Puerto Rico | nil |
| Florida cane | 19 |
| Louisiana cane | 24 |
| Hawaii | 23 |
| Beet area | 35 |
| Total | 101 |

The estimate of net income gains to agricultural resources of approximately $100 million may be compared to the middle cost estimate for consumers and taxpayers of $616 million. Of this total, $418 million was the estimate of the gross transfer for domestic production, with the remainder being a transfer to foreign producers.

The net annual losses from abandoning the sugar program and adopting free trade would be greater than the net annual economic benefits. There are many resources that are now earning only the return that they would earn if they were employed elsewhere. Some of the resources, including both capital and labor, would suffer short-term losses if they had to find alternative uses. Much of the machinery used in sugar cane production, especially the harvesting machinery, has no reasonable alternative use. Management skills especially adapted to sugar production would be reduced in value.

The above estimates do not take into account the income gains to sugar processors. If sugar production in the domestic areas were substantially reduced, much of the capital now invested in raw cane mills and sugar beet refining plants would be of little or no value. It is uncertain whether the sugar refining plants would be able to compete with imported refined sugar if there were free trade. This uncertainty arises because the sugar refineries have been protected by rigid import quotas for several decades. The value added in sugar processing in 1970 was $792 million, of which $252 million represented wages and salaries paid. Cane sugar refiners accounted for nearly half of the value added, but for only 40 percent of the salaries and wages. If the cane sugar refiners are efficient and, thus, competitive, there should be little or no loss of income or capital value. If not, the losses could be substantial.

CHAPTER VIII

# ALTERNATIVES TO CURRENT U.S. SUGAR POLICY

Our present sugar policy has little to commend it. It involves a conflict with our general policy of trade liberalization, particularly the effort to eliminate the use of quantitative restrictions—import quotas. The costs of the program are substantially in excess of the net benefits to domestic producers and all those involved in refining sugar. The operation of our program, along with similar programs of other nations, results in wild gyrations in the international market for sugar. The program maintains high-cost sugar production in the United States while restricting the possibilities of expanding production where sugar can be produced more cheaply.

It is true that the program transfers significant amounts of income to foreign producers. However, there is little rationale behind such a distribution, even if it is viewed as foreign aid. For example, Australia, hardly a needy country, receives fairly substantial benefits from our sugar program.

But it is incorrect to view our sugar program as foreign aid. The higher price received in the U.S. market becomes one of the components in the average return to producers who have quotas to sell to us. To the extent that such producers expand production until their marginal costs equal the expected average price from sales to all markets, there is not a substantial net gain to them. Because so much of the world sugar market is subject to quota arrangements, there would be a loss of employment and income to a given country if it lost its quota to the U.S. market—but there would be no net loss compared to a situation in which the U.S. market were open on a competitive basis.

If there is any long-term benefit to foreigners from our sugar program, it is primarily to governments or consumers in countries that obtain a significant fraction of their sugar on the world market. While there are a number of low-income countries who purchase sugar in the world market, the two largest importers are Canada and Japan. It hardly seems an appropriate national policy objective that we should subsidize Japanese and Canadian sugar consumption. But this is what we *have* been doing. Our policy has lowered the average price of sugar in the world market. Even if all of the countries who purchased sugar in the world market were low-income countries, such an approach to distributing foreign aid—on the basis of the quantity of sugar imports—has nothing to commend it.

## An Adequate Supply of Sugar

A new sugar policy should provide the United States with a supply of sugar such that demand will be met at a price to consumers lower than the price which would prevail with a continuation of the existing program. One of the arguments for the current sugar program is that it is designed to "assure U.S. consumers of a plentiful and stable supply of sugar at reasonable prices." A related argument is that the program makes "it possible, as a matter of national security, to produce a substantial part of our sugar requirements within the United States." [1]

Even though sugar is the source of approximately 17 percent of our total caloric intake, I find it hard to justify classifying it as a product that warrants protection on national security grounds. But equally important, if we produced little or no sugar domestically, most of our sugar supplies would come from the American continent. In case of war, if we could not protect the shipping lanes for sugar from the American continent we would be in a bad way, indeed. It might be argued that in case of a war it would be undesirable to devote the necessary amount of shipping to import sugar, but it can also be argued that the resources that would otherwise be devoted to domestic sugar production would be available for a contribution to the war effort. Basically, the security argument is a specious argument, an argument that is trotted out when there is no suitable rational argument to be made.

In 1960, after the decision had been made to break trade relations with Cuba, a careful review of the potential sugar supply of the United States was made by a U.S. Department of Agriculture special study group at the request of the House Committee on Agriculture. While this study is now almost thirteen years old, some of its pertinent conclusions concerning the availability of imported sugar have stood the test of time so well that its conclusions still appear relevant.

One conclusion of the study is particularly relevant: "It seems clear that from a supply viewpoint the U.S. economy could reasonably expect to fulfill its sugar requirements at significantly lower prices in the decade ahead than the prices that have prevailed in the recent past." [2] In 1959 the quota premium was 2.38 cents per pound and the price for shipment to the United States was 5.35 cents. Three projections of foreign and domestic supply were made for 1970, all assuming no imports from Cuba. The projections were for prices at the 1959 level for shipment to the U.S. (5.35 cents per pound), at twenty-five cents below that level, and twenty-five cents above it. In each case projections were made for supplies from foreign and domestic sources. Actual U.S. consumption in 1970 was 11 million tons of raw sugar. The projections (in millions of tons) were as follows: [3]

|  | Foreign | Domestic | Total |
|---|---|---|---|
| 1959 real price | 8.7 | 8.0 | 16.7 |
| 25 percent above | 11.0 | 13.0 | 24.0 |
| 25 percent below | 6.3 | 3.0 | 9.3 |

According to these projections a world price of sugar between 75 and 100 percent of the 1959 real U.S. price of raw sugar would have provided adequate sugar supplies. Of the imported supply of 8.7 million tons at the 1959 real sugar price, about three-fourths would have come from Central and South American countries.

In fact the real price for sugar shipped to the United States increased between 1959 and 1970. The increase in U.S. wholesale prices was 16 percent, while the price for sugar shipped to the United States increased by 27 percent. Consequently the projection of the domestic supply for 1970 was an overestimate, for actual domestic production was 6.2 million tons, though production could have been somewhat higher if there had been no restraints on mainland cane production and had more sugar beet factories been established.

In his projections of the sources of sugar supply for 1970, Bates projected that only 12 percent of the sugar would come from outside the Western Hemisphere—and this was in the model that excluded trade with Cuba. [4] Under these projections, if there were trade with Cuba, *all* of the imported sugar would come from the Western Hemisphere.

Specific evidence of the response of foreign sugar suppliers was provided by our experience after the cessation of imports from Cuba.

The last full year of Cuban sugar imports was 1959. In that year foreign countries other than Cuba and the Philippines shipped 279,000 tons to the United States. Cuba shipped 3,215,000 tons. By 1961 the other foreign countries shipped 2,945,000 tons to the U.S., and would have shipped more if it had been possible to do so.[5] In 1972 the other foreign countries shipped 3,900,000 tons.

There is enormous potential for the expansion of sugar cane production in Brazil. The word "enormous" is used advisedly. As an example of the potential, it was concluded in 1964 that sugar production in Brazil should be freed from state control, and farmers were permitted to plant any amount of sugar cane they desired. In that year Brazil's sugar cane output was 64 million metric tons. If all the sugar cane produced in 1965 had been harvested, it has been estimated that output would have reached 90 million tons.[6] In the major producing state, Sao Paulo, actual output was 42 million tons and 13 million tons were left unharvested—a total of 55 million tons. Total output increased to 90 million tons in 1972. This represents a doubling since 1956.

After a careful review of the possibilities of expanding sugar production in Brazil, R. M. Paiva, S. Schattan, and C. F. T. de Freitas concluded:

> It can, thus, be seen that, in terms of ecological viability, Brazil possesses an enormous potential and could probably set up more efficient plantations than those now in operation. The economic problem of the limitation of the international market (resulting from import limitations and other factors) has, however, fundamental importance for any attempt to extend or transfer sugar production to new regions.[7]

They also noted that sugar cane production in the Amazon region might well be lower cost than in any of the existing Brazilian producing regions.[8]

Colombia is apparently another low-cost producer of sugar in this hemisphere. Of the sugar that it exports, in recent years more than half has gone to the world market. In 1968 the average price of its exports of raw sugar was less than $60 per metric ton, whereas the price per metric ton for sugar shipped to the U.S. market was $145.[9] In that year Colombia shipped almost twice as much sugar to the world market as to the U.S.—yet its sugar production doubled between the period 1961-65 and 1972.[10]

An adequate supply of sugar would be forthcoming for the United States even if no sugar were produced domestically. If the United States opened its market there would be a shift in sources of supply from those we now rely upon. We have encouraged production in some high-cost areas by providing a protected market for a significant share of output. But we have also excluded additional production from low-cost areas, such as Colombia and Brazil.

## Price Stability

One of the arguments made for the current sugar program is that it has provided a considerable degree of price stability. And it is true that the U.S. program *has* achieved an almost stable real price of sugar for the past decade or more. The supply of sugar is adjusted to meet a specified price objective, and only once since 1962 (in 1963) has there been a significant departure from the objective.

Canada has a sugar policy that merits consideration, at least as a transition measure, for the United States. Under that policy raw sugar is subject to an most-favored-nation duty of 1.287 cents per pound and a Commonwealth preferential duty of 0.287 cents per pound. Domestic producers of sugar beets are guaranteed returns comparable to those received by U.S. producers. However, consumers have access to sugar at the world price plus the tariff. For the period 1963-71 the Canadian wholesale price of refined sugar averaged 8.84 cents per pound, while the U.S. price averaged 11.09 cents—a difference of 2.25 cents per pound or 25 percent of the Canadian price. During that period the highest annual price in Canada was 16.75 cents (3.69 cents above the U.S. price in the same year) and the lowest was 5.65 cents (3.95 cents below the U.S. price in the same year). In one study it was concluded: "It is doubtful whether sugar consumers—householders as well as food manufacturers who account for 70 percent of U.S. sugar distribution—would accept this (Canadian) degree of price uncertainty." [11] In my opinion, such a statement is nonsense. For a difference of 2.25 cents per pound it is possible to accept a rather considerable amount of price variability. It may be true that consumers and other users of sugar prefer price stability to price instability, if the stability can be achieved at no cost.[12] But I do not see how anyone can argue that the Canadian consumer has suffered very much in return for an average saving of about 20 percent.

But we should not complain too loudly about price instability in the world sugar market. After all, our sugar program and similar policies of other industrial countries contribute very significantly to the price instability that has existed. If the world market were the outlet for a fifth or a quarter of world sugar production rather than an eighth, prices would be substantially more stable for the reasons outlined above. Consequently the amount of price variability that has existed in Canada over the past decade is not an accurate indication of what price variability would be if the American market were not so rigidly regulated and our prices could react to prices that reflect demand and supply conditions.

## Long-Run Sugar Policy

Our long-run sugar policy should move toward free trade for both raw and refined sugar. I do not necessarily mean that there should be absolute free trade in sugar, at least not until we have free trade generally. Thus if the national average level of nominal protection provided by tariffs is 10 percent, as it is approximately, the nominal protection provided for both raw and refined sugar should be 10 percent.

The present American tariff rate of 0.625 cents per pound of raw sugar has been higher than 10 percent over the past decade. But if the industrial countries reduced their barriers to sugar imports, the resulting increase in world market sugar prices—perhaps six cents per pound—might make the current U.S. tariff close to the appropriate one.

There is at present no direct tariff protection of refined sugar. A tariff rate that provided 10 percent nominal protection for refined sugar would fall in the range of 0.95 to 1.05 cents per pound. As an alternative to the current virtual prohibition on refined sugar imports, there should be no difficulty in obtaining ready agreement for increasing the import duty on refined sugar from its present rate of 0.625 cents per pound to 0.95 to 1.05 cents. (The above discussion assumes that the 0.5 cent excise tax would be eliminated. It is a protective device in that most of the proceeds are distributed to domestic producers.)

Because most of the crops that compete with sugar beets and sugar cane have price supports, and because price supports established at prices somewhat below the expected market prices can aid farmers in making decisions, I believe that there should be a price support for sugar at the farm level. In order to minimize interference with international trade and the domestic market for sugar, the difference between the price support—now called the target price in the wheat, cotton, and feed grain programs—and actual market prices should be paid as a deficiency payment. Deficiency payments have two added advantages: They make it clear what the program is costing taxpayers, and they make it obvious when price supports are set at levels that encourage uneconomic output.

The price support or guarantee should be set at a level that is no higher than the long-run expected price of sugar cane or sugar beets. In other words, the price commitment should not be used to reintroduce protection of domestic sugar production in another form. In fact, very little would be gained in expanding international trade or reducing the costs to consumers and taxpayers if the present sugar program were modified by eliminating the import quotas, retaining the price objectives of the present legislation, and paying the difference between that price objective and the market price in the form of a deficiency payment. Imports would increase only slightly since the price elasticity of demand for sugar is low, and thus consumption would not be increased very much by the lower consumer price. The use of the deficiency payment would assure the domestic producers prior or first access to the U.S. market. So far as the volume and value of sugar imports are concerned, the critical aspect of the current sugar program is the encouragement of domestic production through relatively high prices. If the same prices were assured with deficiency payments under a target price system, imports could increase by no more than the increase in consumption due to lower consumer prices. Since the current program has limited the output of the mainland cane area, it is possible that the increased output in that area could meet a large part or all of the greater consumption. Thus imports might not increase at all, and the shift to a target price system, with the current price objectives, might result in a larger volume of high-cost sugar production than the present program.

The current price objective, as established by section 201 of the Sugar Act of 1948, as amended in October 1971, maintains the U.S. real price of raw sugar at its level for the period September 1970 through August 1971. The average price of 8.55 cents per pound for raw sugar is moved forward by the average of two indexes, the farm parity index and the wholesale price index. If the same price objective were used to determine the target price, the form of the sugar program would be changed, but not the substance. To be fair, it should be noted that if the target price were set at the price objective as currently defined, and if the payments now paid were eliminated, producer returns would be reduced by about 10 percent.

I want to emphasize again that the sugar import quotas could be eliminated with no significant increase in imports, *if* the present system is replaced by a high enough target price met by deficiency payments. The critical feature of such a program is the level of the target price, not the mechanics of how that price is met. While I would agree that eliminating the sugar quota system would be meritorious, the long-run benefits to foreign sugar producers or to U.S. consumers and taxpayers would be modest at best.

The price support (or target price) should be for sugar cane and sugar beets, not for raw sugar. Putting the price support on raw sugar as the present program does would provide an unknown degree of protection for domestic sugar cane mills and sugar beet processors. In any case, there can only be a calculated equivalent of the price of raw sugar for sugar beets since the processing of sugar beets into sugar is a single-stage process. There would be difficulties in determining the amount of deficiency payments for the fully integrated sugar plantations where the sugar cane is grown and the raw sugar is produced under the same management and ownership. But this hurdle can be surmounted by basing any payments upon the relationships between market prices and the support level in another area.

### The Transition

The sugar program is no different than any other program that has encouraged uneconomic or high-cost production. There is no painless way to end it. Over four decades, investment has been encouraged, human resources have become committed, and expectations have been created in response to the program. On the whole, so far as domestic producers are concerned, the revisions in the program have served only to encourage additional output and created relatively firm expectations that the program will be continued. This is clearly shown by the expansion of sugar cane production in Florida, the establishment of new production areas in Texas and in the Red River Valley over the past two or three years, and the fact that the two newest sugar beet refineries approved for Minnesota and North Dakota (both to be constructed and operated by farmer-owned cooperatives) will be in operation for the first time in 1974.

There are two general approaches to ending programs which encourage uneconomic production: (1) a gradual transition extending over a period of time long enough to substantially depreciate the reproducible capital and to permit a gradual transfer of other resources, and (2) an immediate termination of the program coupled with a concerted effort to adequately compensate those who suffer losses.

The first approach is subject to the possibility that the transition program would become more or less permanent. The second approach is not one that a democracy finds easy to accept. While in the case of the sugar program I think the second approach is the most suitable in terms of minimizing resource waste and consumer costs, the major elements of both approaches are presented below.

**A Gradual Transition.** A gradual transition could include the following major components:

1. Eliminate import quotas, domestic marketing allocations and proportionate shares.

2. Establish target prices based on the price objectives established by section 201 of the Sugar Act of 1948, as amended in October 1971.

3. Make deficiency payments based on the difference between the target prices and actual market prices on a level of output no greater than the average output of the past three years for each producer of sugar cane or sugar beets (this level of production being defined as the "base amount").

4. Continue Sugar Act payments to sugar producers on the base amount for a period of three years, ultimately eliminating the payments through two equal reductions at the end of five years. The excise tax on sugar should be maintained at 0.5 cents per pound during the first three years and then reduced at the same rate as the Sugar Act payments. The Sugar Act payments would be in addition to the deficiency payments required by the target price.

5. During the transition period, producers of sugar and sugar beets should be permitted to abandon cane and beet production in whole or in part and continue to receive the same payments, including both deficiency and Sugar Act payments, as if they had produced the base amount.

The transition program described above would permit a gradual increase in imports, would limit total costs to taxpayers since any increase in output above the base amount for each producer would not generate support payments, and would permit high-cost producers to shift to other productive activity during the transition period without a significant loss of income during that period. If a producer accepted the alternative of producing less sugar than permitted by the base amount, while still collecting payments, the base amount for that form should be reduced if the transition period were later extended beyond five years.

**The Cost of Adequate Compensation.** The second approach for ending the current costly sugar program is to move at once to the long-run sugar program outlined earlier and to pay adequate compensation for all economic losses that would be incurred as a result. As I hope to show, the cost of generous compensation would be little more than the expected total cost to consumers and taxpayers of the continuation of the present program for a period of approximately four years. Since it is assumed that under the long-run program the tariff on raw sugar would remain at 0.625 cents per pound, the additional cost to consumers and taxpayers for the continuation of the current program compared to the long-run program would be approximately $2.14 billion. The upper limit of the compensation for all economic losses is estimated at $2.25 billion. (Most of the assumptions used in arriving at these upper limit estimates are designed to exaggerate the losses.) The more carefully calculated, but still generous, level of compensation set forth below comes to $2.1 billion.

In estimating the upper limit of compensation, it was assumed that all workers now engaged in sugar production would be paid a full year's wage or salary as compensation for displacement. This would cost about $500 million. If the upper limit estimate of net annual income gain to sugar cane and beet producers of approximately $100 million is capitalized at 10 percent, the one-time payment would be $1 billion.[13] A rough approximation of the value of machinery and equipment used on farms to produce sugar is $500 million, even though a significant fraction of the equipment (especially that used for sugar beets) would have value in alternative uses. These estimates are based on new equipment, and if actual equipment were half depreciated, the net loss could not be more than $250 million.[14]

I was unsuccessful in finding an estimate of the total value of structures and equipment invested in sugar processing and refining. An approximation based on value added minus wages and salaries paid indicates an upper limit estimate of less than $1 billion as of 1973.[15] A second approximation, based on information contained in the balance sheets of processing and refining firms that are publicly held, comes out about the same.[16] Both estimates include the investment in facilities to refine raw cane sugar, which may be as much as half of the total investment in processing and refining. Thus no more than $500 million would be required to compensate the loss on investment in sugar beet and sugar cane processing mills.

If it is assumed that the cane refining industry could survive with a moderate rate of protection, the total cost of generous compensation would be no more than $2.1 billion. Approximately a fifth of total wages and salaries in the sugar industry are in cane sugar refining. All of the estimates used in arriving at the $2.1 billion cost can be described as upper limit estimates. More careful investigation of the losses that would be involved probably would result in a substantially lower estimate.

The rough approximations of the full compensation that would be required for ending the current sugar program and moving toward free trade indicate that the savings to consumers and taxpayers would cover the cost in four years. These rough approximations also indicate how large the gross income transfers are relative to the net gains from the program. It is very expensive to encourage high-cost production.

As was noted above, I believe that it would be preferable to end the sugar program immediately and pay compensation to workers and other resource owners rather than using a transitional approach of gradually reducing price incentives. The costs to consumers and taxpayers would be less under a compensation program. However, the United States has never had sufficient political consensus to provide adequate mechanisms for this sort of approach. Thus if we are to eliminate the wasteful sugar program, the only politically feasible alternative may be an extended transition period, perhaps running twice as long as the five-year transition program outlined above. If this longer period is adopted, there should be a gradual reduction in the price objectives as specified in the Sugar Act of 1948, as amended. The rate at which the price objective would be reduced is clearly an arbitrary matter. A reduction in the real price of raw sugar of 3 to 4 percent annually over the five additional years might be sufficient to achieve the long-run policy suggested above.

## Interests of Foreign Producers

As the sugar program now operates, foreign producers with sugar quotas receive the U.S. market price of raw sugar minus the tariff duty of 0.625 cents per pound. The magnitude of the average gain for those countries now having quotas if the long-run policy described above were put into effect is subject to some uncertainty. An increase in the world price of sugar to $120 per ton was projected as the middle estimate in the analysis of costs in Chapter VI. Based on the 1972 long-run conditions assumed in that exercise, foreign producers would receive $160 per ton from quota sales to the United States and perhaps $80 per ton for sugar sold on the world market. In 1972 these countries sold about 5.4 million tons under the U.S. quota systems and approximately 3 million tons to the world market.[17] Admittedly, I do not have a firm basis for estimating the volume of U.S. sugar imports under the long-run program. However, assuming U.S. sugar consumption at 12 million tons, the minimum level of imports might be 10 million tons.

At the prices indicated, which should be considered only rough approximations, the average return to foreign producers would fall from $131 per ton under a continuation of the present program to $120 per ton. If all of the output now sold in the free market were shifted to the U.S. market, it would be necessary to produce 1.6 million tons more in order to meet U.S. import demand.

At first glance these results seem incongruous. There are two reasons why they are not. First, there are a number of low-cost producers who could significantly expand production at a raw sugar price of $120 per ton who now are precluded from doing so by the various preferential systems and the expected low world market price. Second, the world price of raw sugar would increase to $120 per ton and the low-cost producers could expand output in terms of that price. If the sugar producers who have quotas increased their output by 1.6 million tons in the present market situation, their marginal return would be less than $80 per ton and the average return probably less than $120 per ton.[18]

Clearly some of the high-cost producers would lose if the United States adopted the long-run program I have proposed. But I can see no more merit in our encouraging high-cost production in foreign countries than in encouraging it at home. We have benefitted such producers in the past at the expense of low-cost producers elsewhere. We have no responsibility to continue to do so.

# NOTES

## NOTES TO CHAPTER I

[1] Cited in Roy A. Ballinger, *A History of Sugar Marketing*, Economic Research Service, U.S. Department of Agriculture, Agricultural Economic Report No. 197 (Washington, D. C.: Government Printing Office, 1971), p. 5.

[2] Economic Research Service, U.S. Department of Agriculture, *National Food Situation*, November 1973, p. 15. Sugar consumption for 1822 is from Ballinger, *History of Sugar Marketing*, p. 7.

[3] Economic Research Service, *National Food Situation*, p. 15.

[4] Ibid., p. 27.

[5] Ibid, pp. 12, 15.

[6] International Sugar Organization, *Sugar Year Book* (London, 1971), pp. 354-355.

[7] *The World Sugar Economy Structure and Policies: National Sugar Economies and Policies*, vol. 1 (London: International Sugar Council, 1963). An excellent history of the development of sugar production and trade is provided in vol. 2, *The World Sugar Economy Structure and Policies: The World Picture.*

[8] *The World Picture*, p. 13.

[9] Ibid., p. 24.

[10] Ballinger, *History of Sugar Marketing*, pp. 14-16.

[11] Ibid., pp. 6, 122.

[12] Ibid., p. 11.

[13] U.S. Congress, House of Representatives, Committee on Agriculture, *The United States Sugar Program*, 91st Congress, 2d session, 31 December 1970, p. 30.

[14] Ibid., p. 11.

## NOTES TO CHAPTER II

[1] U.S. Congress, Senate, Committee on Finance, *To Include Sugar Beets and Sugarcane as Basic Agricultural Commodities Under the Agricultural Adjustment Act*, Hearings, 73d Congress, 2d session, 1934, p. 3.

[2] House Committee on Agriculture, *United States Sugar Program*, pp. 45-68.

[3] Agricultural Stabilization and Conservation Service, U.S. Department of Agriculture, *Sugar Reports*, August 1972, p. 9.

[4] Ibid.

[5] *Sugar Reports*, December 1972, pp. 6-7. The total of the basic quotas for the domestic beet area, Hawaii, and Puerto Rico was 5,765,000 tons.

## NOTES TO CHAPTER III

[1] *Sugar Year Book*, 1971, pp. 316-322. The published total of world exports (raw value) was adjusted downward to reflect shipments to the U.S. mainland from Hawaii and Puerto Rico.

[2] K. A. Ingersent, "Sugar Export Prices" (Paper presented at 15th International Congress of Agricultural Economists in Sao Paulo, Brazil, 1973), p. 1.

3 Economic Research Service, U.S. Department of Agriculture, *Indices of Agricultural Production for the Western Hemisphere,* ERS-Foreign 264, revised April 1973, pp. 13, 25.

4 When raw sugar is processed in the United States, whether from foreign or domestic services, an excise tax of 0.5 cents per pound of raw sugar is imposed.

5 Ingersent, "Sugar Export Prices," pp. 2-5.

6 Ballinger, *History of Sugar Marketing,* p. 29.

7 Ibid., p. 37.

8 Ibid., p. 30.

9 Ibid., p. 40.

10 Ibid., pp. 40, 42, 65, 67-69.

11 House Committee on Agriculture, *United States Sugar Program,* p. 14.

12 Ballinger, *History of Sugar Marketing,* pp. 69-70.

13 Ibid., p. 71.

14 Ibid., p. 72.

15 Agricultural Stabilization and Conservation Service, U.S. Department of Agriculture, *Sugar Statistics and Related Data,* Stat. Bulletin No. 293, September 1961, p. 152.

16 U.S. Congress, House of Representatives, Committee on Agriculture, *The Development of Foreign Sugar Quotas in H.R. 11135,* 89th Congress, 1st session, 12 October 1965, pp. 5-6.

17 U.S. Congress, Senate, Committee on Finance, *Sugar Act Amendments of 1971,* Hearings, 92d Congress, 1st session, 1971 (two parts), p. 46; hereinafter cited as *Senate Hearings.*

18 Economic Research Service, U.S. Department of Agriculture, *The Western Hemisphere Agricultural Situation,* ERS-Foreign 187, May 1967, p. 47, and ERS-Foreign 351, April 1973, p. 26.

19 These tonnages refer to shipments to the mainland; sugar production was somewhat higher to cover local consumption.

# NOTES TO CHAPTER IV

1 U.S. Congress, House of Representatives, Committee on Agriculture, *To Include Sugar Beets and Sugarcane as Basic Agricultural Commodities Under the Agricultural Adjustment Act,* Hearings, 73d Congress, 2d session, 1934 (Serial J), p. 169.

2 Testimony of Mr. John E. Snyder, ibid., pp. 223-233.

3 Bureau of the Census, U.S. Department of Commerce, *Statistical Abstract* (Washington, D. C.: Government Printing Office, 1947), p. 730.

4 Myer Lynsky, *Sugar Economics, Statistics, and Documents* (New York: United States Cane Sugar Refiners' Association, 1938), p. 9.

5 Ballinger, *History of Sugar Marketing,* p. 40.

6 U.S. Congress, Senate, Committee on Finance, *Sugar,* Hearings, 75th Congress, 1st session, August 1937, pp. 119-120.

7 Ibid., p. 132.

8 *Sugar Reports,* March 1973, p. 8.

9 *Agricultural Trade and the Proposed Round of Multilateral Negotiations* (Report prepared at the request of Peter Flanigan, assistant to the President for international affairs, for the Council on International Economic Policy, printed by Senate Committee on Agriculture and Forestry, 93d Congress, 1st session, 30 April 1973), p. 210.

10 Ibid., p. 223.

11 Ibid.

# NOTES TO CHAPTER V

[1] *Senate Hearings*, p. 50.

[2] House Committee on Agriculture, *United States Sugar Program*, pp. 18, 50.

[3] U.S. Congress, House of Representatives, Committee on Agriculture, *Extension of the Sugar Act*, Hearings, 92d Congress, 1st session, 1971 (Serial 92-E), p. 400; hereinafter cited as *House Hearings*.

[4] *Senate Hearings*, p. 60.

[5] *Sugar Reports*, August 1972, p. 24. The Dominican Republic could have shipped more sugar to the United States since it sold sugar on the world market in 1970—almost 30 percent as much as was shipped to the United States; *Sugar Year Book*, 1971, pp. 318, 366.

[6] House Committee on Agriculture, *United States Sugar Program*, p. 63.

[7] *Senate Hearings*, p. 53.

[8] Ibid., pp. 32-33.

[9] *Sugar Reports*, January 1973, p. 10.

[10] Ibid.

[11] *Sugar Reports*, August 1972, p. 8.

[12] *Senate Hearings*, p. 153.

[13] *House Hearings*, pp. 730-731.

[14] The output approximation was made by assuming that the average payment rate per hundredweight of raw sugar for the largest farms was about two-thirds of the average for all farms.

# NOTES TO CHAPTER VI

[1] The price elasticity of −0.2 is a rather rough estimate based on results presented by Thomas H. Bates, "The Long-Run Efficiency of United States Sugar Policy," *American Journal of Agricultural Economics*, vol. 50, no. 3 (August 1968), p. 531. If the price elasticity were as high as −0.4, which seems highly unlikely, the increase in consumers' surplus would be $38.5 million instead of $15 million with an elasticity of −0.2.

[2] *Senate Hearings*, p. 66.

[3] House Committee on Agriculture, *United States Sugar Program*, p. 53.

[4] *Sugar Year Book*, 1971, pp. 306-315.

[5] Ingersent, "Sugar Export Prices," pp. 3, 5.

[6] House Committee on Agriculture, *United States Sugar Program*, pp. 52-53.

[7] *Sugar Year Book*, 1971, p. 305. The average is for 1968 through 1971.

[8] *Journal of Commerce*, December 5, 1973.

[9] The projections of world sugar prices used for the estimates of the U.S. sugar program are intended to represent average prices for the sugar cycle, not price peaks or troughs.

[10] R. W. Snape, "Some Effects of Protection in the World Sugar Industry," *Economica*, vol. 30 (February 1963), p. 66.

[11] Bates, "The Long-Run Efficiency of U.S. Sugar Policy," p. 531.

[12] Food and Agricultural Organization of the United Nations, *A World Price Equilibrium Model* (Rome, 1972), p. 23.

[13] U.S. Department of Agriculture, *Agricultural Trade and the Proposed Round of Trade Negotiations* (Washington, D. C.: Government Printing Office, 1973), p. 227.

[14] It is assumed that the cost of transportation from the greater-Caribbean ports to the United States is 0.5 cents per pound of raw sugar.

# NOTES TO CHAPTER VII

[1] Economic Research Service, U.S. Department of Agriculture, *Farm Income Situation*, July 1973, pp. 38, 64, and *Sugar Reports*, April 1973, p. 24.

[2] The estimates of the prices received by farmers for the raw sugar content of cane and beets are for mainland production only. The estimates were made from data on the sugar processed per ton of sugar cane and sugar beets; *Sugar Reports*, January and February 1973, and Statistical Reporting Service, Crop Reporting Board, U.S. Department of Agriculture, *Crop Production*, 8 June 1973, pp. 22-23.

[3] The estimate of the sugar production on 224 farms is based on the distribution of the acreages of sugar cane planted (acres harvested for sugar and seed and bona fide acreage abandoned) published in *Sugar Reports*. The latest data for Hawaii are for 1966. For the other three areas the data are for 1971. The estimated production is for farms with 500 or more acres of sugar cane and were calculated by estimating the acreage planted on farms with 500 or more acres as a residual. It was assumed that output was proportional to acreage. The data were from the following issues of *Sugar Reports*: April 1967, January 1973 and April 1973.

[4] The conclusion that the net income benefits from producing sugar beets will be capitalized into the price of land assumes that farmers act rationally in allocating their resources. And I do believe that farmers do act rationally. What acting rationally means is that at the margin the return to all mobile resources such as farm machinery, fertilizer and labor are the same in the production activities. Thus there remains only one resource to which the additional income, if any, can be attached and this is land. If there are no significant restraints on the amount of land that a farmer can devote to the production of sugar beets, there would be no additional net income to attribute to the production of sugar beets.

[5] For the new plants authorized in 1962, see Ballinger, *History of Sugar Marketing*, p. 71. For data on plants operating in 1972, see *Sugar Reports*, October 1972, pp. 19-23. For changes in acreages of sugar beets in Arizona, see Table 8 in this chapter.

[6] *Sugar Reports*, October 1973, p. 8.

[7] U.S. Department of Agriculture, *Agricultural Statistics* (Washington, D. C.: Government Printing Office, 1972), p. 554.

[8] U.S. Department of Agriculture, Special Study Group on Sugar, *Special Study on Sugar*, House Committee on Agriculture, 87th Congress, 1st session, 14 February 1961, p. 89.

[9] *Sugar Reports*, March 1973, p. 9.

[10] F. J. Hills and S. S. Johnson, *The Sugar Beet Industry in California*, California Agricultural Experiment Station and Extension Service, Circular 562 (Berkeley: University of California, 1973), p. 10.

[11] Robert A. Young, *An Economic Study of the Eastern Beet Sugar Industry*, Michigan State University Agricultural Experiment Station, Research Bulletin 9 (East Lansing: Michigan State University, 1965), p. 40.

[12] *Sugar y Azucar*, November 1973, p. 31.

[13] Bureau of the Census, *1969 Census of Agriculture*, vol. 1, "State Reports."

[14] *Sugar Reports*, April 1973, pp. 23-24, and August 1972, pp. 25-26.

[15] *Sugar Reports*, August 1972, pp. 27-28.

[16] Bureau of the Census, *1969 Census of Agriculture*, vol. 1, part 50, "Hawaii," p. 18.

[17] Sugar cane prices are not published for Hawaii, apparently because most of the sugar cane is processed by the same firm that produces the cane.

[18] House Committee on Agriculture, *United States Sugar Program*, p. 65.

[19] *Sugar Reports*, August 1972, pp. 25-28.

[20] *House Hearings*, pp. 37, 39.

[21] Sugar Act of 1948, as amended (1971), Title II, sec. 202(a)(3).
[22] Sugar y Azucar, March 1972, p. 30.
[23] Ibid., January 1972, p. 27.
[24] Ibid., February 1973, p. 29.
[25] Ibid., June 1972, p. 45.
[26] Ibid., July 1973, p. 33.
[27] See Sugar Reports, August 1972, p. 26, for production and other issues for annual quotas.
[28] Bureau of the Census, 1969 Census of Agriculture, vol. 1, "State Reports," part 29, "Florida," and part 35, "Louisiana."
[29] Ibid., part 35, "Louisiana."
[30] Sugar y Azucar, June 1972, p. 33.
[31] Ibid.
[32] Sugar Reports, January 1973, pp. 25-26.
[33] The number of landlords was estimated by subtracting the number of farms from the number of payees and is thus only approximate. Some farms could have more than one operator.
[34] Sugar Reports, January 1973, p. 25.

# NOTES TO CHAPTER VIII

[1] House Committee on Agriculture, United States Sugar Program, p. 29.
[2] Special Study on Sugar, p. 4.
[3] Ibid., pp. 2-4 and 64.
[4] Bates, "Long-Run Efficiency of U.S. Sugar Policy," p. 531.
[5] House Committee on Agriculture, United States Sugar Program, p. 14.
[6] Ruy Miller Paiva, Salomao Schattan and Claus F. Trench de Freitas, Brazil's Agricultural Sector: Economic Behavior, Problems and Possibilities (Sao Paulo: 15th International Conference of Agricultural Economists, 1973), p. 170.
[7] Ibid., p. 173.
[8] Ibid.
[9] Ingersent, "Sugar Export Prices," p. 3.
[10] House Committee on Agriculture, United States Sugar Program, p. 53, and Economic Research Service, U.S. Department of Agriculture, Indices of Agricultural Production for the Western Hemisphere, ERS-Foreign 264, revised April 1973, p. 15.
[11] Agricultural Trade and the Proposed Round of Multilateral Negotiations, p. 228.
[12] Obviously price stability does involve a cost, either through the costs of storage or, as in the case of the sugar program, a highly managed domestic market for sugar. One aspect of the managed market has been a relatively high price for sugar.
[13] The estimated value of the loss of land value due to the elimination of the sugar program may be compared with the increase in the value of farm real estate (in forty-eight states) of $58 billion between 1969 and 1973. Source: Economic Research Service, U.S. Department of Agriculture, Balance Sheet of the Farming Sector, AIB 365, October 1973, p. 32.
[14] The approximation to the value of farm machinery and equipment used for sugar cultivation are based on data in Hills and Johnson, The Sugar Beet Industry in California, p. 9, and House Hearings, p. 774. Almost all of the machinery used for sugar beet production can be used for other crops.
[15] Bureau of the Census, Statistical Abstract of the United States, 1972, provides an estimate of the net value of equipment and structures in all manufacturing for 1970 in 1958 dollars (p. 700). The total was $124.0 billion. If this

figure is adjusted upward by the increase in the cost of building construction index (ibid., p. 677) of approximately 60 percent, the value of equipment and structures in 1970 dollars is estimated at $198 billion. This is clearly on the high side since equipment represents about 60 percent of the net value of equipment and structures and equipment prices rose much less than construction costs between 1958 and 1970. Value added in all manufacturing in 1970 was $298.3 billion (ibid., p. 697) and in the sugar industry, $0.815 billion. In all manufacturing a dollar of value added was associated with $0.66 of equipment and structures in 1970. If the same relationship prevailed for sugar processing and refining, the value of equipment and structures used in sugar manufacturing would have been $538 million.

[16] Data from *Moody's Industrial Manual* indicate that investment in property and equipment per ton of sugar processed ranges from $60 to $100 per ton. A third approach gave a general estimate of the value of assets consistent with the other two approaches. Data were obtained from *Moody's Industrial Manual* for nine publicly held companies that were substantially involved in sugar processing. The data were for a fiscal year that ended some time during 1972. Net profits were calculated as a percentage of sales. The range was from 0.7 percent to 5.0 percent with most being in the range of 1.5 to 2.5 percent. For refined sugar, either cane or beet, a net profit of 2.5 percent would be 0.3 cents per pound of sugar; for raw sugar processing the net profit would be about 0.25 cents per pound. In 1972 the total quantity of refined sugar processed was 11.4 million tons and the profit on this quantity would be $67.4 million; the quantity of raw sugar was 2.8 million tons and the profit on this quantity would be $14.0 million. The total profit, assuming the same profit rate on sugar processing as on all other activities of the firms involved, may be estimated at $81.4 million. Assuming a 10 percent rate of return the implied value of net assets is $814 million. This figure is somewhat high since a number of the firms were also producers of sugar cane and the profits on that production have been included in the total.

[17] *Sugar Year Book,* 1972, pp. 335-340, 387-388.

[18] If sales on the world market were increased by 1.6 million tons over the recent quantities of about 8 million tons, the increase in supply in that market would be about 20 percent. Given the nature of that residual market, the decline in price would be substantial.